WALKING WITH
LONDONERS
400 YEARS IN 12 WALKS

TIM POTTER

Walking with Londoners: 400 Years in 12 Walks
Copyright © 2023 Tim Potter
All rights reserved.

Tim Potter asserts the right to be identified as the author of this work in accordance with the Copyright, Designs and Patents Act 1988. All rights reserved. No part of this publication may be reproduced, stored in a retrieval system, or transmitted, in any form or by any means, without the prior permission of the copyright owner.

Book cover and design by Sadie Butterworth-Jones
www.luneviewpublishing.co.uk

Maps by Alan Boyd

ACKNOWLEDGEMENTS

To Alan for the maps.

Sadie for the design.

Isabell, Anastasia and others for photographs.

Steve, Ann, Cath for proof reading.

And to Tracy, Matt, Sarah and Adam.

CONTENTS

Introduction 7

1. Oliver Cromwell and Charles I: Regicide, Republic and Restoration 9

2. Samuel Pepys and the Industrial Thames 21

3. Christopher Wren and the Rebuilding of London 37

4. Alexander Pope and the Arcadian Thames 53

5. The Brunels in London 65

6. Charles Dickens and Victorian London 77

7. Karl Marx and the Streets of Soho and Bloomsbury 91

8. Bazalgette and the Transformation of London 105

9. The Lammins of Orchard Place 121

10. The Suffragettes: From Outsiders to Westminster 133

11. The Women of Bow 149

12. The Salters of Bermondsey 163

About the Author 178

INTRODUCTION

In this book I explore the history of London through the lives of Londoners. We cover four hundred years by walking with a dozen or so people who made London their home. They all transformed the city, sometimes the country, and in a few cases the world. Some of our figures are internationally known; revolutionaries in their fields of politics, architecture, literature or engineering. Some of the others, though, are much less well known. The Salters are still remembered but mainly in Bermondsey and few people know of Minnie Lansbury. And then there are the Lammins of Orchard Place. Very few people know about them or the area in which they lived and yet, for us, they can represent the ordinary, nameless generations of Londoners: the ones who, through their labour, built our city.

London's history is complex and can be divisive. Few of these Londoners would be seen as truly great today. Cromwell, for instance, remains hated by many for his war of conquest in Ireland. Dickens left his wife in the most brutal way and took up with a 17-year-old actress. Pepys committed what can only be described as rape. Emmeline Pankhurst was dictatorial with the suffragette movement and awful to her own children. (She sent one of her daughters a one way ticket to Australia and never saw her again.) But despite their flaws, these individuals also made history. They had vision. Cromwell to execute a king. Bazalgette to transform a city's infrastructure. Marx to change the way the world thought. And all this was done here in London.

These individuals represent our history and by walking with them you're walking through our history. If you walk in the footsteps of Cromwell, Pepys and Wren you hopefully get a flavour of the turbulent years of the 17th century. Walking with Marx and Dickens should help you visualise the poverty and squalor of 19th century England while with Bazalgette and Brunel you'll realise the grandeur of the Victorians' vision. Or walk with Annie Besant, Sylvia Pankhurst and Ada Salter and I hope it helps you understand the passion and commitment of these women whose work led to mass trade unions, the National Health Service and the vote.

Of course, all this has great relevance to our own age.

Marx, the Brunels and Minnie Lansbury's parents probably wouldn't be let into Britain under current asylum rules. On the most basic level, it's impossible to write about Bazalgette and the Great Stink of 1858 without remembering that today water companies are dumping raw sewage into our rivers and seas on a daily basis. Writing about Ada Salter's housing schemes or Alfred Salter's revolutionary healthcare brings to mind the tragedy of Grenfell or the current crisis in the NHS.

Our history informs our present. I hope this book raises some challenging questions: the debate between ends and means, the role of the individual, the way we conveniently airbrush out of history the bits we don't want to see. And, indeed, how reputations can rise and fall as we review figures from the past through our own experience.

A word of warning: to get the most out of this book you're going to need your imagination and lots of it. To see 21st century Deptford through Samuel Pepys' eyes is a pretty heroic feat. Sometimes, I'm going to ask the almost impossible; we're going to walk through Whitehall and Westminster twice. The first time as a Cromwellian revolutionary in 1649 and then as a suffragette with Emmeline Pankhurst in 1910. The same buildings but with different eyes. It can be done – promise!

By living in or visiting London we have been handed an extraordinary historical legacy. I hope this book, like its predecessor, 'Walking London's History', opens up a little more of that past for a few more people and, together, we continue to preserve it for our allotted time.

1. OLIVER CROMWELL AND CHARLES I: ROYALTY, REGICIDE AND RESTORATION

Westminster and Royal London are on every tourist's itinerary. Deservedly so — the buildings are known throughout the world. It has been at the centre of English and then British power for a 1000 years. History permeates this small area. In fact, there is so much history there that it can be difficult to make sense of what you're looking at.

So, a quick, potted history of Westminster. The story dates back to 600 AD when monks set up a small monastery on the Isle of Thorney, a muddy island by the Thames. 400 years later, Edward the Confessor rebuilt the abbey there. In 1066 he died just as his church was completed and he became the first of many monarchs to be buried there. William the Conqueror was then crowned in the abbey, the start of an almost unbroken line of coronations lasting for the next 1000 years. When a great new Cathedral was built in 1269, Westminster's pre-eminence in the life of the country was confirmed.

By the 14th century, a Royal Palace of Westminster had emerged and this attracted other great nobles to build houses near the river to be close to royal power, such as the palace of the Archbishops of York in London. When Thomas Wolsey, Henry VIII's right hand man, became the Archbishop he set about transforming it into the luxurious White Hall Palace. But Wolsey fell and Henry, along with his new wife, Anne Boleyn, moved in. Under the extravagant Henry, the Palace blossomed to become the greatest in the land.

The heyday of Whitehall Palace lasted until the 1690's when two catastrophic fires broke out within the space of just 7 years. The monarchs moved out and the politicians took over. Walpole, the first recognisable prime minister, was gifted 10 Downing Street as his official residence and around this house the machinery of government grew.

In this walk we're going to concentrate on one particular period in this long history: an era where the clash of ideas about God, government and the state led to civil war and the death of a king. We will be walking in the footsteps of Charles I and Oliver Cromwell during the middle of the 17th century.

Neither of the two were Londoners. Charles I was born in Dunfermline to the Scottish King, James VI of Scotland, who became James I of England after Elizabeth I's death. Cromwell was born in Huntingdon, a moderately wealthy farmer and land-owner. Both however died at Whitehall, Charles on the executioner's block, Oliver as de facto dictator of England.

The roots of the conflict between Crown and Parliament had been growing for years. Charles believed in the divine right of kings: the right to rule absolutely without reference to others. But he needed money and for that he needed parliament which also wanted a stake in the government of England. There were also religious differences across society with much dissatisfaction at the monopolistic Church of England. The country was split between those who wanted greater freedom for Catholics to worship (one of the motivations behind Guy Fawkes and the Gunpowder Plot) and those who wanted less religious control by the Church of England to practice a more Puritan, truly Protestant faith.

Matters came to a head in 1642 when Charles I tried to arrest MPs who disagreed with him. When he was thwarted, he raised the royal standard to mobilise the country against parliament. Within a few weeks both sides could boast sizeable armies. A bloody Civil War played out, with England torn apart. Cromwell became a leading general for the Parliamentary cause and created the New Model Army, a powerful and professional force. This led to the king's armies being decisively broken at the battle of Naseby in 1645. Charles became the prisoner of Parliament and the army. Despite his defeat, Charles continued to foment plots, encouraging supporters to relaunch the war. Royalist risings took place in Wales, Southern England and Scotland. By now, Cromwell was the leading military and political figure on the parliamentary side. He was determined to end the conflict and led demands for the trial and execution of the king. Charles was duly executed on 30 January 1649.

The war was not yet over. The royal banner was taken up by the future Charles II, the executed king's son, but within two years, his armies, too, had been crushed and he was forced into exile in France. Cromwell was appointed Lord Protector and by 1653 took up residence in the royal palace of Whitehall. For the first and only time in its history, England was a republic. Cromwell's rule lasted until his death five years later.

By this point, Parliament and the Army were riven with factions and exhausted by nearly two decades of unprecedented turmoil. General Monk, leader of Parliament's

Scottish Army, marched south, took control of Parliament and opened negotiations with Charles II to take the throne. On 29 May 1660, Charles II returned to London as king.

While Charles was merciless with those who had signed his father's death warrant, in general he was more tolerant of political and religious differences. Conflict was quelled, but the power of Parliament and Protestantism remained. When Charles's brother, James II, a Catholic, came to the throne, he was removed in the so-called Glorious Revolution of 1688. From then on, the crown was subject to parliament.

London was at the heart of this great conflict. It was solid in its support for Parliament against the king and provided more troops for the parliamentary forces than any other region. These times are some of the most tumultuous that London has lived through and they have divided historians ever since. For some, this was an un-English, extremist episode which cuts across their view of the pragmatic and evolutionary course of the country's history. For others, it was a turning point of modern history which led eventually to the creation of a parliamentary democracy with a monarchy limited to providing a bit of glitter to the constitution.

The key protagonists, too, are divisive. For many years, there was a cult of Charles I, the Martyr. It was said that miracles were performed in his name and 3000 masses were said annually for his soul. Many modern historians, however, see him as a vain, weak, stubborn and ineffective ruler unable to understand or adapt to the changes within society. Cromwell is even more divisive. While he was named in the top 10 of the greatest ever Britons in a BBC poll in 2002, he remains deeply controversial. For some, he is the hero of parliamentary democracy and the man who destroyed the *'divine right of kings'*, but for others, he is a monster. Certainly, his campaign to subjugate Ireland led to the deaths of perhaps 40% of the population. The memory of the massacre at Drogheda is slow to fade. And yet, his statue stands outside the House of Commons and, for many, Cromwell remains the father of English democracy.

FURTHER READING

Whitehall: The Street that Shaped a Nation, by Colin Brown

Cromwell: Chief of Men, by Antonia Fraser

THE WALK

In this walk we discover the 1000 years of history behind modern Westminster and Whitehall but, in particular, we trace the arena of the great clash between Crown and Parliament in the 17th century. We will walk where Charles and Cromwell once walked, and discover what is left from that time.

This walk is always beautiful, but St James's Park is at its very best from April to June.

1. Eleanor Cross
2. Charles I Statue
3. Whitehall Palace
4. Banqueting House
5. Horse Guards
6. Downing Street
7. Westminster Hall
8. Oliver Cromwell Statue
9. Westminster School
10. St James's Park
11. St James's Palace

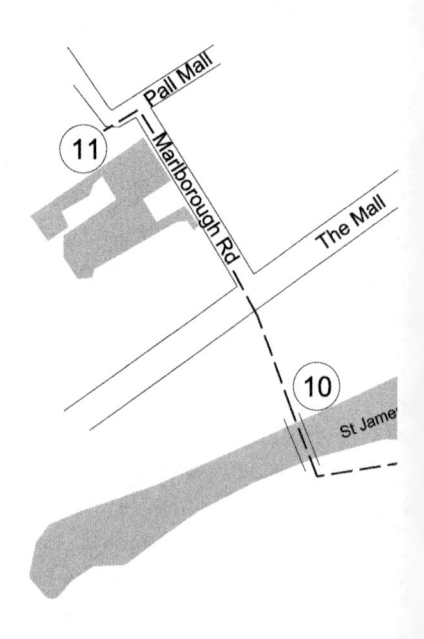

1. Oliver Cromwell and Charles I

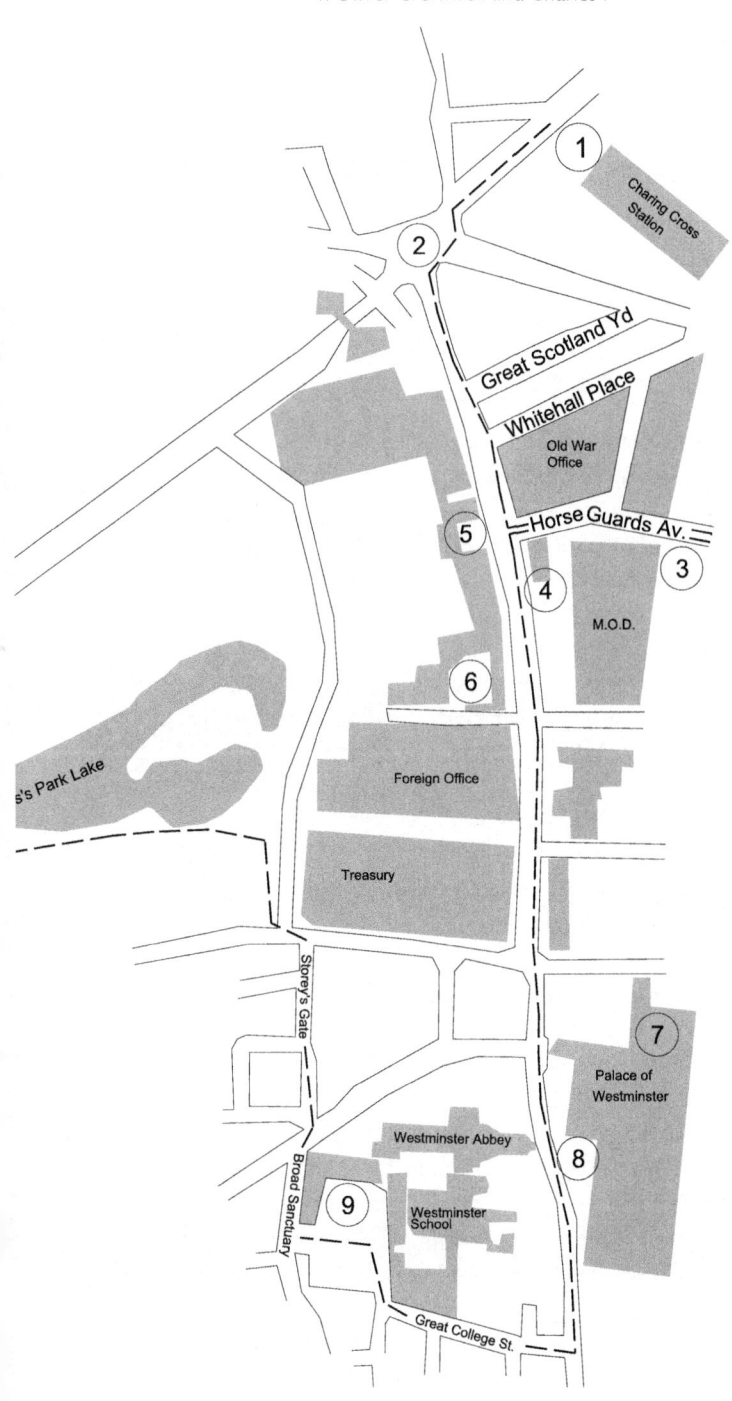

THE ROUTE

We start outside Charing Cross Station on Strand (that's its official name, although everyone calls it the Strand). The name Strand is one of the few reminders of Anglo-Saxon London. Strand is Anglo Saxon for beach, and this used to be where the old town (or Aldwych) met the river over a thousand years ago. Charing, too, is derived from an Anglo-Saxon word meaning a bend in the river.

Stop 1
We start by the great monument in the taxi rank of Charing Cross Station on the Strand. The monument is the Eleanor Cross, which commemorates Eleanor of Castile, wife of Edward I, who died in 1290. The heartbroken king built 12 impressive crosses to mark where her body rested on her final journey back to Westminster Abbey. (Please, do not feel too upset for the mourning King. He was also the 'Hammer of the Scots', conqueror of the Welsh and persecutor of the Jews.)

The monument in front of you is not original, however. Nor is it on its original spot. The original was pulled down as idolatrous by the Parliamentary forces during the Civil War. What you see today is Victorian and only erected in 1865.

Walk left along the Strand towards Trafalgar Square and cross the road to the equestrian statue marooned on the traffic island.

Stop 2
The statue is of Charles I, gazing down Whitehall towards Banqueting House, his place of execution. This was originally where the Eleanor Cross stood. After it was pulled down, the site remained bare for three decades. This spread alarm amongst some Londoners, as a contemporary ballad recorded:

Undone! Undone! The lawyers cry, they ramble up and down; they know not the way to Westminster, now Charing Cross is down.

After the Restoration, the statue of Charles re-emerged, having been hidden by royalist sympathisers. It was placed here in the very centre of London and, traditionally, it is where distances from London are measured. It was also where many of the those who signed the death sentence of Charles I were executed. Most famously, perhaps, Major General Thomas Harrison was hanged, drawn and quartered here in 1660. Samuel Pepys wrote in his diary that Harrison was *'looking as cheerful as any man could do in that condition.'*

Walk down Whitehall, passing on your left Great Scotland Yard where emissaries of the Scottish Crown would stay when they were visiting the English Monarch, then turn left down Horse Guards Avenue. You are now at the entrance of the Old Whitehall Palace, which is buried beneath your feet. Pass in front of the entrance to the imposing Ministry of Defence. Built in the 1930's, it's redolent of the bombastic architecture of those Britain fought in the Second World War. At the gardens at the end of the street are the only visible remains of Wren's Palace of Whitehall.

Stop 3

The great palace of Whitehall, as built by Cardinal Wolsey and lived in by Henry VIII, was all but destroyed by two devastating fires in 1691, and again in 1698. After the first, Christopher Wren was commissioned to rebuild the palace but, after the second fire, work was abandoned. The king, William III, moved out of Whitehall and got Wren to develop a new palace on the edge of town. It's what we now call Kensington Palace.

Look over the low wall and you'll see a series of steps leading down into what was once the river entrance to the palace. This is all that's left of Wren's work.

Today, this river entrance is 100 yards or so from the Thames. We'll see why in the chapter on Bazalgette later. Some parts of Wolsey's Palace still remain but are buried deep underground. His wine cellar is underneath the Ministry of Defence, and across Whitehall there are remnants of Henry VIII's cock-fighting pit and his tennis court. But these are out of bounds to visitors, except on very rare occasions.

Retrace your steps to return to Whitehall and stop by one of the most magnificent buildings in London.

Stop 4

This is Banqueting House, built by Inigo Jones in 1622 as the centrepiece for the Stuart dynasty. It, along with the Queen's House in Greenwich, introduced the new neo-classical architecture into London, where it rapidly swept away the fanciful Tudor style. Based on the rigid rules of Palladio in Northern Italy, the new architecture was based on the classical architecture of Greece and Rome, on symmetry and the rational application of architectural principle.

Banqueting House was the centre of the Stuart Palace of Whitehall. The roof of its great hall is decorated with a spectacular painting by Rubens extolling the achievements of the Stuarts. It is ironic then that this was also the site of the execution of Charles I. On 30 January 1649, Charles stepped out on to a makeshift stage where his head was separated from his shoulders.

Look up and you'll see a bust of Charles staring balefully down and a plaque telling us that he stepped out of a nearby window to his death.

Nearby, there is a second, less well known memorial to his death. Cross Whitehall to stand outside Horse Guards.

Stop 5

The building you see dates from 1759, but it replaced one from 1663. This is the HQ of the Household Cavalry, set up by Charles II in 1660 to act as the King's Personal Bodyguard. Their base was at the entrance of Whitehall Palace, protecting the monarch when he was in residence. Clearly, Charles II didn't want to face the same fate as his father, and based his crack troops there for his protection. The whole building housed a more important function for nearly 200 years, serving as the centre of the British Army until the 1850's.

Now look up at the clock at the top of the centre of the building. You'll see there's a black spot at 2 o'clock. Why? Because Charles I was executed at 2 in the afternoon, and it is a symbol of mourning for the dead king.

Walk down Whitehall until you reach perhaps the most famous address in London – Downing Street.

Stop 6

The street, famous as the official residence of the Prime Minister and Chancellor of the Exchequer, is named after one of the most notorious characters of the Civil War and Restoration: George Downing. He lived an extraordinary life; brought up in Massachusetts, he was the first graduate, and then first professional tutor at Harvard. He returned to England before the Civil War and became Cromwell's Scout Master, or spy catcher, in Scotland. He supported the execution of Charles I and extended his spy-catching to uncovering Royalist plots in the Netherlands. However, after Cromwell's death, he switched allegiance to Charles II and became HIS spy catcher, hunting down his erstwhile comrades who had signed Charles I's death warrant. The regicides were seized and smuggled out of the Netherlands to be executed in London as traitors. His reward was handsome: he was knighted and given a prime piece of land on the edge of Whitehall Palace. He called on Christopher Wren to design the houses in what is now called Downing Street. Downing went on to have an illustrious career as a diplomat. He was, for instance, responsible for negotiating the transfer of New York from the Dutch in 1674. However, his reputation as a turncoat never left him. Pepys called him *'a perfidious rogue.'*

Carry on walking down Whitehall. Downing Street marks the southern edge of the Palace of Whitehall. Very soon you will enter the boundaries of the Palace of Westminster. As you walk towards Westminster you pass first the Foreign Office, with its sculptures and inscriptions detailing the supposed benefits of belonging to the British Empire, and then the Treasury. When you get to the end of Whitehall, cross to the left and then cross Bridge Street so that you are standing on the corner staring up at Big Ben (or more properly, the Elizabeth Tower.)

Stop 7

While Big Ben is spectacular, we are much more interested in the building nestling at its foot: Westminster Hall.

Built in 1099 by the son of William the Conqueror, it was then probably the largest hall in Europe. It was the site of the first and earliest forms of Parliament, when Simon de Montfort brought representatives from the provinces together in 1265. It was also where some of the most important state trials in English history have taken place: of William Wallace, Guy Fawkes and Sir Thomas More. It's not surprising that they were all found guilty and executed. For our purposes though, the most important trial was of Charles I, by judges appointed by Parliament. His trial lasted a week, even though the king refused to recognise the court's authority. The outcome was a foregone conclusion; the court ruled that:

'This court doth adjudge that the said Charles Stuart, as a tyrant, traitor, murderer and public enemy to the good people of the nation, shall be put to death, by the severing of his head from his body.' Three days later, the executioner did just that.

11 years later, in 1660, Westminster Hall became the last resting place of the head of Oliver Cromwell. His body had been disinterred from his tomb in Westminster Abbey by the vengeful Charles II, subjected to a mock 'execution' and the head impaled on a spike outside the Hall.

Walk round the front of Parliament until you come to the statue of Oliver Cromwell.

Stop 8

Like many statues in London, this has a very contentious history. It was erected in 1899 but has always been controversial. Its erection was bitterly opposed by Irish Nationalists because of Cromwell's bloody record in the suppression of Ireland. It was also opposed by monarchists, given Cromwell's role as regicide. The controversy lives on: as recently as 2004 a group of MPs tried to have the statue melted down.

The statue portrays Cromwell with eyes cast down, and this has led to a bizarre urban myth. Walk across the road to St Margaret's Church directly opposite the statue. On the right of the church you will see a small bust: it is of Charles I gazing implacably at his executioner. Legend has it that Cromwell could not meet the accusatory stare and so his eyes are cast down. The story is, of course, utter nonsense. Charles's bust was put up in the 1950's, years after Cromwell was placed on his plinth.

Continue walking down St. Margaret Street, passing another reminder of the medieval Palace of Westminster: the Jewel Tower. This was, in effect, the Treasury of the Plantagenets. Early accounting practices give us the word Exchequer; the nation's revenues and expenditures were calculated on a chequered cloth. Turn right down Great College Street, and then turn right through an arch into Deans Yard in the precincts of Westminster School. (Occasionally, this entrance is closed, in which case you'll have to retrace your steps and walk back to Parliament Square to the main door of the Abbey.)

Stop 9

Westminster School could be the oldest school in England, perhaps dating back to before the Norman Conquest. The first written records date to the early 14th century. Old scholars are a very mixed bunch including six prime ministers; scientists like Christopher Wren and Robert Hooke; musicians Andrew Lloyd Webber and Shane McGowan of the Pogues; actor John Gielgud and spy Kim Philby.

Walk through the gate at the far end of the square into Broad Sanctuary. Then cross the road and continue on down Storey's Gate and into St. James's Park. Walk through the park, looking out for the famous pelicans, and then cross the bridge over the lake.

Stop 10

The view from the bridge is tremendous, enclosed by four royal palaces: Whitehall, Westminster, Buckingham and St James's. You can thank Charles II for the view and the pelicans. He opened the park to the public and he received the first pelicans from the Russian ambassador in 1664. Before then the area had been enclosed by Henry VIII as yet another deer park for his personal entertainment.

Carry on walking over the bridge, out of the park, cross the Mall and up Marlborough Road. You are now walking along the side of St. James's Palace. This had been a women's leper hospital. By the way, the names of both the Mall and Pall Mall derive from a game a bit like croquet, which was fashionable in the 17th century. Walk up to Pall Mall and turn left to the front of the palace.

Stop 11

St James's Palace is a fine example of Tudor architecture. Built by Henry VIII in 1531 as a bolthole from the more formal Whitehall Palace, it became a favourite royal residence for the next 150 years. Mary I died there and Charles II, James II, Mary II and Queen Anne were all born there. St. James's reached the peak of its importance during the 18th century and is regarded as the 'senior' royal palace. Even today, ambassadors are accredited to the Court of St. James. Most importantly for our story, it was also the place where Charles I spent his last night before being escorted down the park to his execution at the Banqueting House. This is an appropriate place to end our walk.

AND FINALLY

There are a few pubs scattered amongst the clubs, galleries and restaurants in St. James's, but perhaps you could retrace the steps of the doomed Charles I from the Palace to the Banqueting House and visit one of the many good pubs on Whitehall such as The Old Shades, The Silver Cross or Walkers of Whitehall.

You're close to Green Park station or, if you do walk back to Whitehall, Trafalgar Square and Embankment stations, as well as Charing Cross, are close to hand.

FURTHER EXCURSIONS

If you're interested in Royal London, it's a lovely walk through the parks from St James's, via Buckingham Palace, through to Kensington Palace. If you're feeling more of a republican, then you can visit Cromwell's family house in Ely or the Cromwell Museum in his birthplace of Huntingdon.

2. SAMUEL PEPYS AND THE INDUSTRIAL THAMES

Samuel Pepys is a very well-known name. In fact, so famous that he is taught to six-year-olds in English Primary Schools. His diaries, written between 1660 and 1669, made him one of the great chroniclers of London. His descriptions of the restoration of the monarchy, the terrible plague years and the Great Fire of London are some of the historians' most important sources for that period. His diaries hand down to us not just the events, but the very atmosphere of Restoration London. It was often dark and uncertain, full of unexpected death, with danger lurking round every corner. But it was also the London of Charles II, the 'Merry Monarch', where London escaped from the oppressive rule of Oliver Cromwell and the puritans.

Pepys moved at all levels of Restoration society. He was a frequent visitor to the King at Whitehall, but also drank in the pubs of Fleet Street, flirted with the actresses in the theatres of Covent Garden and worked alongside shipbuilders, carpenters and sailors. He enjoyed the new found freedoms in the city to the full: his diaries are packed with gossip and intrigue and detail Pepys' appetite for music, good conversation, food and drink as well as his illicit sexual encounters. By the way, the last bit is not taught to six-year-olds!

Samuel Pepys was that rare thing; a famous Londoner who was actually born in London. And he was born at its very centre, in Salisbury Court just off Fleet Street, midway between the Tower of London and the King's Court at Whitehall. His family were not wealthy, but they had connections and Samuel was a clever, precocious child. He joined the Civil Service and through ability, aided by patronage, he rose rapidly through the ranks. For most of his working life he was the most important civil servant of the English Navy. His achievements in that role were enormous. He was a brilliant administrator and introduced necessary reforms in the procurement of goods and the selection and training of officers. In effect, he was laying the foundations for a much more efficient Royal Navy that would dominate the waves for the next two hundred years.

During the 1660's, Pepys lived and worked at the Navy Board, close to the Tower of London. He worshipped at the parish church of St. Olave's, almost next to his house. It's still a beautiful medieval church that survived both the Great Fire of 1666 and the Blitz. The area around here is full of buildings that are mentioned in Pepys' diary and were familiar to him in his later life. Much of his working life was spent in Deptford, Greenwich and Woolwich, which were beginning to be the centre of the Navy's operations. Here the great warships were being built, repaired and provisioned. To the east, the Thames was beginning to lose its rural character and was becoming a centre of industry and commerce.

Pepys gave up writing his diary in 1669, fearful that it was harming his eyes. But we no longer need to rely on his words to track the rest of his life. By now he was a very important figure in London and there are plenty of sources to trace his future career. He lived another 34 years, surviving the reigns of Charles II, James II, William and Mary and lived to see Queen Anne on the throne. His long-suffering wife, Elizabeth, did not share in his future success. She died of a fever aged 29 in the same year that the diary ends. She was buried in Samuel's church of St. Olave with a fine memorial. Pepys never remarried, although he had a long relationship with his housekeeper, Mary Skinner.

Politically these were troubled times as Charles II continued to reign without producing a legitimate heir. (He produced plenty of illegitimate ones; at least 12 with seven different mistresses.) This led people to fear that his brother, James, Duke of York and a Catholic, would accede to the throne. Anti-Catholic hysteria rose and, in the paranoid atmosphere, Pepys was accused of treason and imprisoned in the Tower. In total, he managed to end up there three times. As one of the most senior officials in the Navy, any failings in the service could easily be taken as a sign of treachery at the top. But Pepys survived and was very much at home in the top echelons of English Society. He was elected Master of Trinity House, the body responsible for all the inland waters, harbours, maps and lighthouses surrounding the English coast. He became an MP and, in 1684, he was elected president of the Royal Society, the most prestigious scientific body in the world at that time. There he met with the greatest minds of the day such as Christopher Wren, Robert Boyle and Isaac Newton. Indeed, the front cover of Newton's Principia Mathematica, perhaps the most important book in the history of science, bears Pepys' name on the front cover.

One of his closest friends for almost forty years was Sir John Evelyn, a fellow diarist and founder member of the Royal Society. Pepys records how they spent hours gossiping about the latest rumours at court or the art and science of the day. Sometimes they just laughed together. On 10 September 1665 *'Mr Evelyn's reciting of some verses did make us die almost with laughing ... it being one of the times of my life wherein I was the fullest of true sense of joy.'* Not surprisingly, after evenings like this, the two were friends for life. Evelyn lived in a large house with gardens in Deptford, close to the Deptford shipyards, so Pepys would often combine business with pleasure, inspecting work at the shipyards and then being entertained by his friend.

Pepys retired from public life when James fled England in the Glorious Revolution of 1688. He lived in wealthy retirement before dying in 1703. He was buried in front of the altar of St. Olave's under the watchful eyes of his wife's statue. His was a grand funeral attended by the great and good including the Archbishop of Canterbury and the President of the Royal Society: a fitting tribute to a great man of his times. Evelyn wrote in his diary on 26 May 1703 *'This day died Mr. Sam Pepys a very worthy, industrious and curious person ... Mr Pepys had been for neere 40 years so much my particular friend that (I was asked) to hold up the pall for his magnificent obsequies, but my indisposition hinder'd me from doing him this last honour.'* Evelyn's indisposition was serious, by then he was in his eighties and he died a few years later. Thus ended the lives of London's two most famous diarists. Indeed, a whole chapter of London's history was also ending as the Stuart dynasty came to an end and were replaced by the minor German royals, the Hanoverians.

FURTHER READING

For those interested in Pepys' diary, there is an extraordinary website where you can both read and search through the diary. It's **www.Pepysdiary.com**

For the best biography of Pepys, try:

Samuel Pepys: The Unequalled Self, by Claire Tomalin

THE WALK

The walk starts with an amble around the Tower of London through the streets where Pepys lived, worked and worshipped. We then take the boat from Tower Hill to Greenwich, which Pepys often visited. We walk down the south bank of the Thames from Greenwich to Rotherhithe. Along the way we'll see where Peter the Great, Czar of all the Russias, came to visit to study the English Navy. We'll see the remains of the Deptford shipyards where Pepys commissioned new vessels for the English Navy and where he conducted some of his most notorious assignations. We'll see the earliest of the great London Docks and, as an added bonus, see where Christopher Marlowe, the great Elizabethan dramatist, was assassinated.

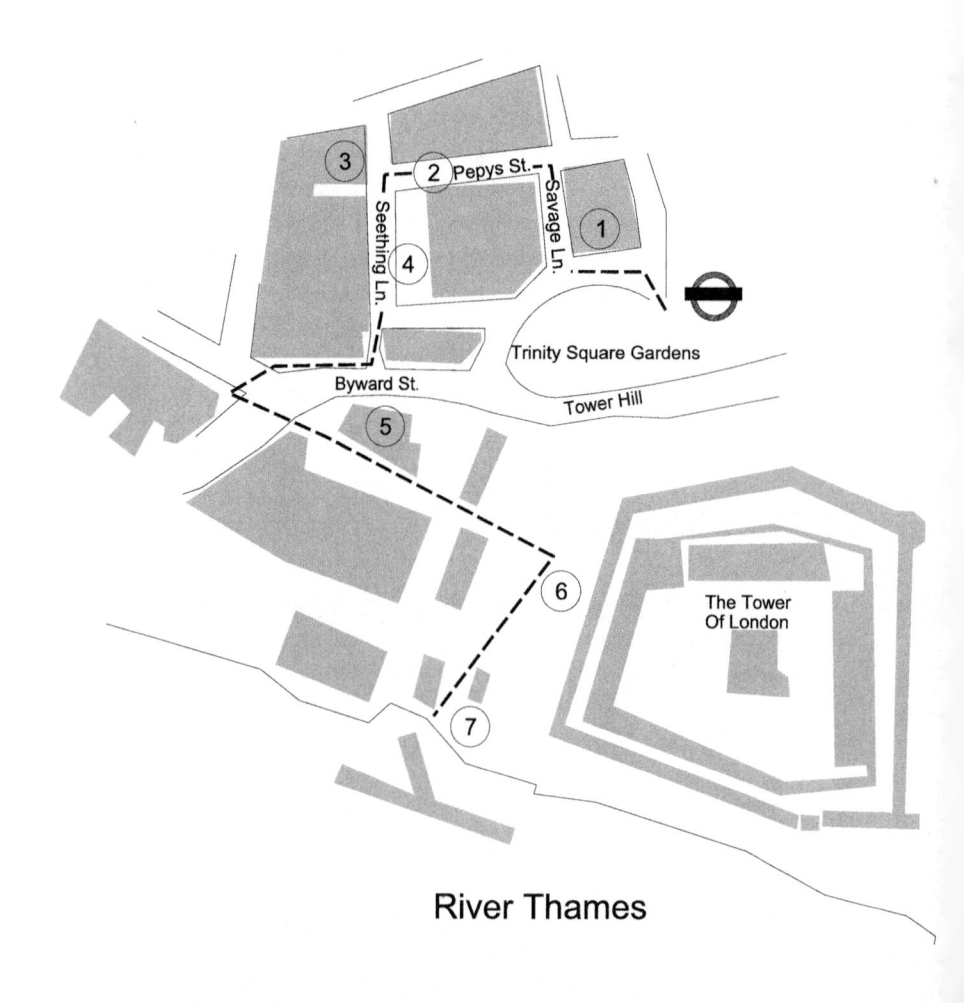

1. Trinity House
2. Pepys Street
3. St Olave's Church
4. Seething Lane Garden
5. All Hallows Church
6. Tower of London
7. Tower Millennium Pier

THE ROUTE

We start in Trinity Square Gardens just by Tower Hill Underground Station.

Stop 1

On the north side of the gardens lies Trinity House. It was set up in 1514 by Henry VIII under the snappy title of 'The Master, Wardens and Assistants of the Guild, Fraternity, or Brotherhood of the most glorious and undivided Trinity, and of St. Clement in the Parish of Deptford-Strond in the County of Kent.' Luckily for everybody, it soon became known just as Trinity House. In 1566, its duties were described as to *'make, erect, and set up such, and so many beacons, marks and signs for the sea... whereby the dangers may be avoided and escaped, and ships the better come into their ports without peril'*. The house in front of you was not the original headquarters. They were based first in Deptford, then Stepney in Pepys' time, later moving to just by All Hallows church. The current building dates from the 1790's. Trinity House was an important and prestigious body as it safeguarded maritime trade for the English ports. So Pepys' election as master of Trinity House was a mark of the important role he played within the maritime community.

Walk past Trinity House and right up Savage Gardens. Turn left onto Pepys Street and walk towards the church on the corner of Seething Lane.

Stop 2

You are now in the very centre of where Pepys lived, worked and worshipped when he was writing the diary. The Navy Office was on Seething Lane just to your left and Pepys lived in a house attached to the Office.

Cross the road into the churchyard, noting the memento mori above the gateway. This dates back to Pepys' time as the churchyard was used as a plague pit in 1665, burying hundreds of people in its grounds. On 30 January 1666, Pepys wrote *'It frighted me indeed to go through the church ... To see so many graves lie so high upon the churchyard, where many people have been buried of the plague.'* On the outside of the church's walls, just to the right of the door, there is a plaque commemorating the fact that Samuel had a private entrance cut into the wall so that he could come from the Navy Office without getting wet and, if he was late, without too many people noticing.

Stop 3

Inside, the church is very beautiful and a precious remnant of the medieval churches that used to dominate the city. Seventy were destroyed in the Great Fire, Victorian urban planning destroyed more, and then the Blitz damaged most of those left. St Olave's was badly damaged in the war but very sympathetically rebuilt. Both Pepys and his wife are buried in the church. High above the altar on the left hand wall is the bust of Elizabeth. Pepys wrote the inscription which included the eulogy *'Gifted with beauty, accomplishments, tongues; she bore no children for she could not have borne her like.'* She was just 29. She looks down sternly on the grave of her husband who was buried alongside her in front of the altar. A Victorian plaque up on the wall to your right remembers Pepys.

Exit the church through the church yard and walk to your right down Seething Lane and, opposite you, is a small green space.

Stop 4

This is Seething Lane Garden and marks the site of both Pepys' house and the Navy Office where he lived.

There is a bust of Pepys in the garden and the pavement is engraved with many of the subjects that made Pepys and his diary famous. This was where, during the Great Fire: *'I did dig another pit and put our wine in it; and my parmezan cheese as well as my wine and other things.'* On the pavements you should spot the cheese as well as the Great Fire, the plague, ships and war, as well as the activities that Pepys loved: music, food and drinking.

Carry on walking to reach Great Tower Street. Cross the street to the charmingly named 'Hung, Drawn and Quartered' pub. It is called this after an entry in Pepys' diary. Cross Lower Thames Street to All Hallows Church.

Stop 5

All Hallows claims to be the oldest church in the City of London, dating back to 675 AD, founded in Saxon times. It was once owned by Barking Abbey so was often referred to as Barking church.

The door under the tower is called Pepys Door for this is where, on the 5 September 1666, at the height of the Great Fire, Pepys wrote:

'About two in the morning my wife calls me up and tells of new cryes of fyre – it being come to Barkeing church which is the bottom of our lane. I up to the top of Barkeing steeple and there saw the saddest sight of desolation that I ever saw. Everywhere great fires. Oyle cellars and brimstone and other things burning. I became afeared to stay there long; and therefore down again as fast as I could.'

It was said that up until the Blitz of 1940 you could still see the scorch marks caused by the Great Fire at the bottom of the church tower.

Bear right round the church across the square, till you are standing opposite the tower.

Stop 6

The Tower of London played a very important role in Pepys' life. It was from here on the first day of the Great Fire that Pepys:

'got up one of the high places and there I did see the houses at that end of the bridge all on fire, and an infinite great fire on this and the other end of the bridge.'

So alarmed was Pepys that he immediately set out from the pier by the Tower to interrupt the King and the Duke of York at prayers to tell them of the extent of the fire. They commanded him to tell the Lord Mayor of London to start pulling down houses to create fire breaks. It didn't do much good because when Pepys found the Mayor *'he cried like a fainting woman, "Lord, what can I do? I am spent: people will not obey me. I have been pulling down houses; but the fire overtakes us faster than we can do it". That he needed no more soldiers ... and must go and refresh himself, having been up all night. So he left me.'* The Lord Mayor wasn't seen again until the fire was safely out.

The Tower was also the scene of Pepys' imprisonment after he was wrongly accused of being implicated in the Popish Plot of 1678 when a wave of anti-Catholic hysteria, whipped up by Titus Oates, swept the country. Hundreds were caught up in the entirely fictitious 'plot' and over 20 people were executed. Pepys was lucky, he was only imprisoned for a few months.

Stop 7
Walk down by the side of the tower and you will see the Tower Millennium Pier. We, like Pepys, are going to take a boat from the tower, but we will travel not to Whitehall, but downstream to Greenwich.

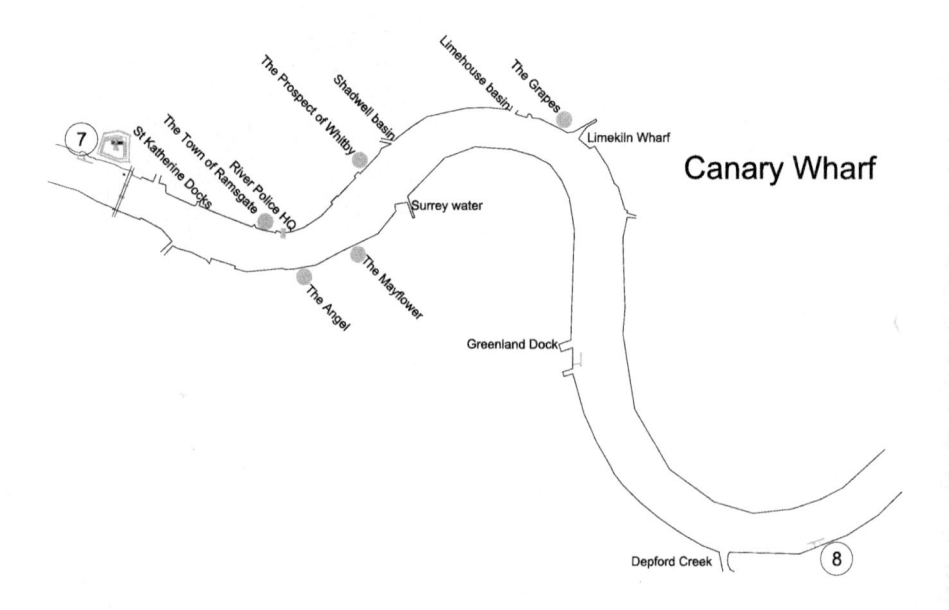

7. Tower Millennium Pier   8. Greenwich

Along the way, we pass the riverside hamlets of Wapping, Bermondsey, Limehouse, Rotherhithe and Deptford. All of these places were visited by Pepys many times to inspect ropeworks and mast houses, to see ships being built or refurbished or to talk to captains in the riverside taverns. You'll see many of the pubs that Pepys used to frequent such as the Town of Ramsgate, The Prospect of Whitby, the Grapes, the Angel and the Mayflower. All these pubs date back to at least the 17th century, though many of their names have been changed since Pepys' time. Pepys' diary also makes clear just how industrialised the Thames was at this time. There are hundreds of references in the diaries mentioning a dozen different places, all producing ships and guns for the King's navy.

Stop 8

Get off the boat at Greenwich Pier and to your left you can see Charles II's great Palace at Greenwich, which later became the Royal Naval Hospital, then the Royal Naval College and today the University of Greenwich. In Pepys' time, the old medieval palace was being rebuilt after it had served as Prisoner of War camp, and then a biscuit factory during the Civil War. When Pepys visited on 16 March 1668, he commented: *'I to Greenwich by water and there landed at the King's House which goes on slow but is very pretty.'*

Behind the Palace is the Royal Observatory, commissioned by Charles II in 1675. Pepys, as a member, and indeed president, of the Royal Society, and as a leading figure in the Navy Office, would have been keenly interested in its development. Its primary purpose being to measure *'the places of the fixed stars so as to find out the so much desired longitude of places for the perfecting of the art of navigation.'*

On leaving the pier, turn right to start walking along the river bank back towards London. On your right you soon pass the Greenwich foot tunnel which replaced the medieval ferry across the river. Today it is used mainly by the tourists who flood in to Greenwich, but originally it was built to enable dockers living in Greenwich to get to the docks quickly and for free.

Within a hundred yards or so there is a small inlet, the remains of the old ferry. Pepys used it many times, often complaining about the amount of time it took him to get over the river.

Keep walking along the river bank and then cross over the footbridge spanning Deptford Creek. This was where the Golden Hind, Francis Drake's ship which circumnavigated the globe, was left to rot. It had been built at Deptford and Queen Elizabeth I had ordered that it be kept safe near where it was built.

Walking with Londoners

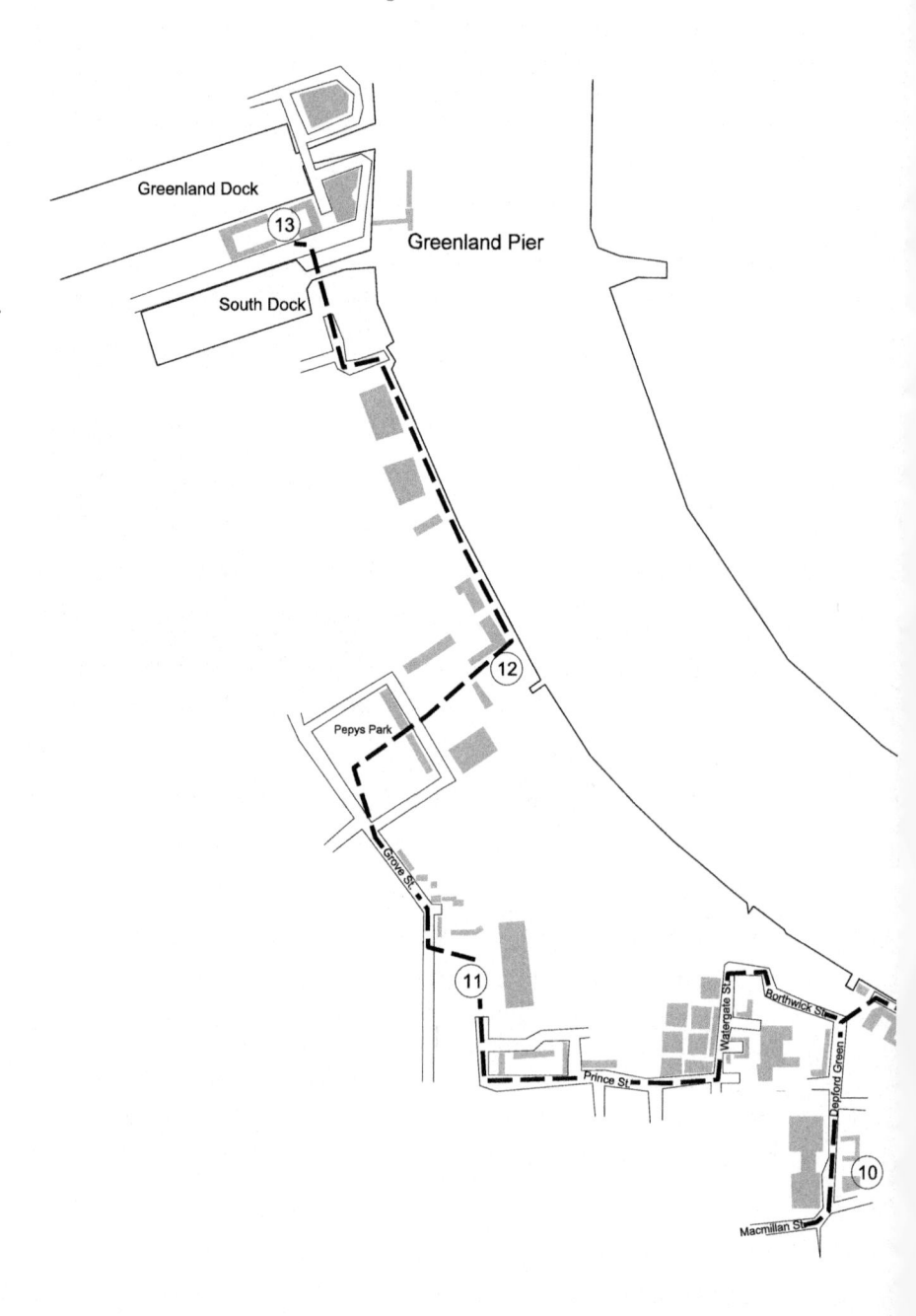

Greenland Dock

(13)

Greenland Pier

South Dock

(12)

Pepys Park

Grove St

(11)

Watergate St

Borthwick St

Prince St

Deptford Green

(10)

Macmillan St

2. Samuel Pepys and the Industrial Thames

8. Greenwich Pier
9. Peter the Great Statue
10. St Nicholas Church
11. Sayes Park
12. Deptford Shipyard
13. Greenland Dock

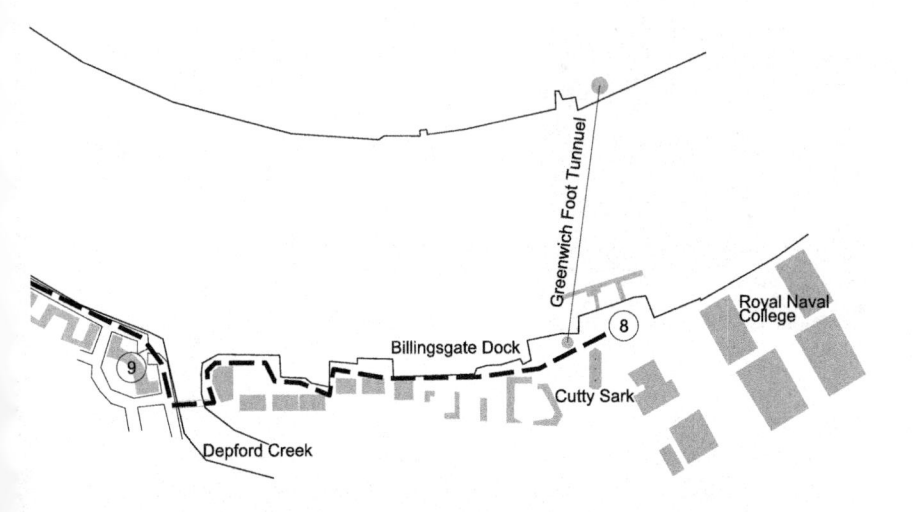

Stop 9

On the opposite bank of Deptford Creek, you come across a very strange statue given as a gift by the Russian state. It is of Peter the Great and commemorates his stay in John Evelyn's house at Sayes Court for four months in 1698. He was there to learn the secrets of English prowess in ship building and so stayed close to the Deptford shipyards. The visit was a diplomatic triumph for England but a financial disaster for John Evelyn. Peter trashed the place, riding horses down the corridors and destroying his gardens.

The statue shows an enormous Peter the Great (in real life he was 6' 8"), with, on his left, a dwarf. In Peter's entourage, there were 4 dwarfs, and the comparison between the giant Peter with his tiny companions was seen as uproariously funny. (At the time of writing the dwarf is covered up due to damage caused by someone trying to steal him for the metal).

Keep walking down the riverside with some great views across the Thames.

At the Ahoy charity, you're forced inland. Walk up Deptford Green to your left and in a few hundred yards you arrive at St. Nicholas Churchyard.

Stop 10

There's been a church on this site since the 12th century, if not well before, but the current church dates from the 18th century. As you walk through the entrance there is another extraordinary Memento Mori on the gate pillars.

Walk around the graveyard. In the opposite corner to the entrance is a memorial to Christopher Marlowe, the great Elizabethan playwright. He was a contemporary of Shakespeare but was murdered in a Deptford riverside tavern when only 29. In his brief life he had already written some theatrical masterpieces such as Dr Faustus, Edward II and Tamburlaine the Great which are still performed today. Officially he died during a drunken argument over the payment of a bill after an afternoon's drinking, but it is more likely he died on the orders of Sir Thomas Walsingham, one of Elizabeth I's spymasters. For Marlowe was a spy operating in the dangerous hinterland between foreign powers and Catholic conspirators. The debate still continues as to why he died.

Exit the graveyard where you came in and look to your left.

This was the heart of Deptford in Pepys' time and it was in the street just in front of you that one of Pepys' long time mistresses, Mrs Bagwell, lived. Then her house was in Flagon Row, now called MacMillan Street. They had an affair for at least 5 years, but one to which Mr Bagwell seems to have agreed. Pepys had promoted the husband to a senior position in the Navy which conveniently led him to being away from London on a regular basis. As a result, it seems that the husband was complicit in, and accepting of the relationship between his wife and his patron. Quite what Mrs Bagwell thought of it is not clear as we only have Pepys' views on the affair.

Mrs Bagwell crops up in the diary many times and the entries include this remarkable and terrible story. To the modern eye, it sounds very much like rape.

On 20 December 1664, Pepys wrote:

'I walked with Bagwell home to his house and there was very kindly used and the poor people did get a dinner for me in their fashion of which I did eat very well. After dinner I found occasion of sending him abroad and then alone 'avec elle je tentais a faire ce que je voudrais et contre sa force, je le faisais biens que passe a mon contentement.' By and by he coming back again I took leave and then walked home.'

There are plenty of other stories like this in the diary, with some women more willing than others. At the very least we would, today, call Pepys a sexual predator if not a rapist.

Retrace your steps till you get to Borthwick Street on the left. Turn left till you reach Watergate Street. In front of you is the old wall of the Deptford shipyards.

If you turn right here it takes you to the river with a fine and unexpected view of the river. To your left behind the wall is the Master Shipwright's House, one of the finest early 18th century houses in London. It hosts art shows and a theatre, but unfortunately you can't visit except for performances.

So instead, turn left down Watergate Street and then right down Prince Street, past the Dog and Bell Pub. At the end of Prince Street turn right down Sayes Court Street until you reach the entrance of Sayes Park.

Stop 11

This is the site of the manor house of Sir John Evelyn; one of Pepys' closest friends. Pepys often came here to see his friend. On 5 May 1665, for instance: *'we walked in his garden, and a lovely noble ground he hath indeed.'* A few months later he wrote: *'Evelyn showed me round his gardens which are for variety of evergreens and hedge of holly, the finest things I ever saw in my life'.* Afterwards, in the coach to Greenwich: *'all the way having fine discourse of trees and the nature of vegetables.'*

In the middle of the grounds is a very old mulberry tree which, it is said, was donated to Evelyn by Czar Peter the Great, perhaps as compensation for trashing his house and garden.

Exit the park at the gate on your left and walk to your right along Grove Street. After 300 yards or so you come on your right to Pepys Park. This is the Lower Pepys Park, walk across it through a gap in the social housing opposite to Upper Pepys Park beyond. Both parks were built on the site of the royal dockyards. The dockyards not only built and repaired the Navy's ships along the river, but they also reprovisioned the ships. This area contained, for instance, a biscuit factory, an abattoir and warehouses used for storing food and drink, especially rum. Apparently just one of the warehouses could hold 32,000 gallons of the stuff.

Walk through the park until you reach the river again and turn left to walk past some fine 18th century offices.

Stop 12

These are the Deptford Shipyards, all that remains of what was once one of the most important centres of the Royal Navy. From the time of Henry VIII, some of the greatest names of the English Navy are associated with this spot. Both Sir Francis Drake and Sir Walter Raleigh were based here when in London. Later, ships such as those used by Captain Cook were built and sailed from these shipyards. The buildings are offices associated with the Victualling Offices for the yards. They include the

Porters' Lodge, some warehouses and the Officers' Houses.

There are some fine ornamental steps leading down to the riverside. According to legend, this is where Elizabeth I came to knight Francis Drake after his circumnavigation of the globe. As she stepped on to the stairs, so Walter Raleigh laid his cloak down for her to step on, thus avoiding muddy shoes. All very unlikely.

Walk a few hundred yards along the riverfront and you soon come to the entrance to an enormous dock complex.

Cross over the first bridge and you arrive at the Greenland Dock Pier for the ferry service back to central London where our walk could end.

Stop 13

Greenland Dock is London's oldest wet dock and was originally built in 1699, 100 years before the great West India Docks. To begin with, it specialised in ship repair and could hold up to 120 ships at any one time. It became known as Greenland Dock in the 18th century as it began to specialise in the whale trade where blubber was rendered down to make whale oil. When this trade declined it concentrated on the lumber trade and some 80% of all wood imported in to London passed through these docks.

Today it is devoted solely to recreation and is a nice place to sit and watch the water. If you're looking for a place to rest, a few hundred yards up the north side of the dock is 'The Moby Dick'. It's a modern building but with great views over the docks.

AND FINALLY

To get home, you've got two main options.

I've already suggested taking the ferry back into Central London from the pier we passed at Stop 13. Or it's a 15 minute walk to Canada Water Station on the Jubilee and Overground lines. To get there, keep walking up the north side of the dock until you reach the end and go under a red swing bridge. You're following the line of an old canal, but in a hundred yards you hit a shopping centre. Follow it round and in a few hundred yards you'll come to Canada Water Station.

FURTHER EXCURSIONS

A wonderful day out would be to visit Pepys' library at Magdalen College in Oxford. The library contains Pepys' collection of 3,000 books, including the famous diary, housed in bookcases designed by Samuel in 1666. It's open most days between 2 and 4 but do check before you go at **www.magd.cam.ac.uk**

3. CHRISTOPHER WREN AND THE REBUILDING OF LONDON

INTRODUCTION

Christopher Wren had more impact on the fabric of London than any other single architect in history. He's best known for his reconstruction of the City of London after the Great Fire of 1666 where he rebuilt 51 of the 70 churches destroyed. In addition, he built some of the great public buildings of the time, including the Chelsea Hospital, the Royal Naval Hospital in Greenwich, and Kensington Palace. These great works dominated, defined and shaped London for the next 300 years.

Like most of the 'Londoners' in this book, Wren was not born in London but in Wiltshire in 1632. He seems to have attended Westminster School briefly as a boy before going up to Oxford where he was introduced to some of the leading mathematicians and scientists of the day. London was to become his home for most of his exceptionally long life; he eventually died in St. James's at the age of 90.

Wren today is primarily known as an architect but he was much, much more than that. He was also a physicist, an astronomer and a mathematician. His first major post was as Professor of Astronomy at London's Gresham College where he gave weekly lectures on science. These conversations attracted the cream of Restoration London's intelligentsia and eventually led to the creation of the Royal Society in 1660. Its foundation really marked the beginning of the English Enlightenment with its explosion in scientific knowledge. The Society's motto, *'Nullius in Verba'*, meaning *'Take No-One's Word for It'*, sums up the revolutionary challenge to received and accepted thinking. Wren went on to be president of the Royal Society, as did Samuel Pepys and Isaac Newton. Wren also became the King's Surveyor of Works, responsible, in effect, for all public buildings promoted or owned by the monarch. He was elected as an MP four times and knighted in 1673.

While Wren was mightily successful in his own age, it's his impact on London that has been so long-lasting. As his obituary, inscribed on his tomb in St. Paul's Cathedral stated: *'Here in its foundations, lies the architect of this church and city, Christopher Wren, who lived... not for his own profit but for the public good. Reader, if you seek his monument – look around you.'*

So why was Christopher Wren so important? There are two main reasons: the first is his impact on architecture and the second on religion.

Wren had enthusiastically adopted the new architectural trends developed by Palladio in northern Italy often called Neo-Classicism. These had been introduced into London by Inigo Jones with the building of the Banqueting House in Whitehall and the Queen's House in Greenwich. The rationality of design, the symmetry and precision of these new buildings marked a clear break from the flamboyance of medieval architecture and the homely Tudor style which it replaced. Instead, Neo-classicism was based on the mathematical principles of Renaissance architecture which itself was based on the buildings of ancient Greece and Rome. This new style became the blueprint for most architecture for the next few centuries. It's easily recognised by its use of squares, triangles, arches and ovals and the preponderance of classical columns.

Wren was very much part of this classical style but to it he allied the flamboyance of English Baroque. These softened and enlivened the often austere facades with elaborate and beautifully carved decorations, especially around windows and over arches. The decoration extended into the churches as well. Wood carvers, such as Grinling Gibbons, were commissioned to design beautiful font covers and reredos. Reredos were large wooden panels at the back of the altar which were often inscribed with the founding texts of the Christian faith, at least according to the Church of England.

The popularity of reredos in Wren's churches also reflected the changes in the way people viewed religion in the late 17th century. This is the second reason why Wren was so important. His churches reflected and altered the way people looked at religion, and especially the version practised by the Church of England.

3. Christopher Wren and the Rebuilding of London

The English Reformation, which created the Church of England, was a strange affair; it was as much political as it was religious, and its services reflected the tastes of the time. In the times of Charles I, for instance, it had veered more towards the more Catholic, 'high church' wing, while during the Protestant high point of the Civil War and Protectorate of Oliver Cromwell, it had shifted back towards a more austere, more personal view of religion. These shifts had always taken place, however, in churches whose architecture had been sponsored by the Catholic church. What that meant was that the altar would usually be in a chapel at the eastern end of the church, often slightly separated from parishioners by the choir. The altar was often difficult to see because of the pillared naves, the small stained glass windows and the separation of the chancel from the nave. What this led to was a separation of clergy from the faithful, as well as a sense of mystery, of the importance of faith and reliance on others to lead worship.

The rebuilding programme after the Great Fire gave Wren the opportunity to create a vision of what a Protestant church should look like. A defining feature of Protestantism is perhaps the emphasis on the importance of God's word. This was to be delivered without too much translation by and through the church hierarchy. It was for you, the individual, to hear and ponder on the biblical texts and draw your conclusions from them. So the churches that Wren built are often open with the altar, not tucked away at the end of the church, but more in the centre where all the parishioners could see and understand the services. That's why the reredos were so large and important in his churches, as they were there to proclaim key tenets to the faithful. Wren himself wrote: *'In our reformed religion, it should seem vain to make a Parish church larger, than that all who are present can both hear and see. The Romanists, indeed, may build larger churches, it is enough if they hear the murmur of the Mass and see the elevation of the Host but ours are to be fitted for ... all to hear the service and both to hear distinctly and see the preacher.'*

These new churches were often full of light with enormous pulpits so all could see and listen. One of the things Wren disliked was stained glass. Indeed, this was a bit of a touchstone for Protestants of the time. Stained glass darkened the interior of churches, diverted attention away from the word of God and led to a more mystical atmosphere. Protestantism demanded clarity, rationalism and light. As a result, almost all the stained glass you'll see was added much later, usually in Victorian times. Wren's churches are also notable for their diversity; he was a genius at fitting new churches into old spaces and every church is different.

By 1673, Wren was running a major architectural practice as he struggled to keep up with the avalanche of work that was being generated. This was both repairing the damage caused by the Great Fire, and delivering the many commissions he received, as the Stuart monarchy endeavoured to leave their mark on London. As a result, many other architects were involved through his offices. Nicholas Hawksmoor was the most famous of Wren's protégés. He had started as Wren's apprentice, but by the end of the 17th century was delivering churches and houses on his own account.

Whatever the contribution of others, it is Wren's name that lives on. He really was London's great architect and, as his obituary said, his memorial is all around us.

FURTHER READING

There are several good guides to London's churches such as:

London's City Churches, by Stephen Millar

A Guide to London's Churches, by Mervyn Blatch

Biographies of Christopher Wren include *On a Grander Scale,* by Lisa Jardine

3. Christopher Wren and the Rebuilding of London

THE WALK

This walk is best done on a weekday as many of the churches are not open at the weekend. The churches rely, in the main, on volunteers and can also be unexpectedly closed or hosting services. However, what's great about Wren churches in the city is there's always another one just round the corner. So if some are shut, just go to the next one.

1. St Olave

2. St Dunstan's in the East

3. St Margaret Pattens

4. St Mary at Hill

5. St Magnus the Martyr

6. The Monument

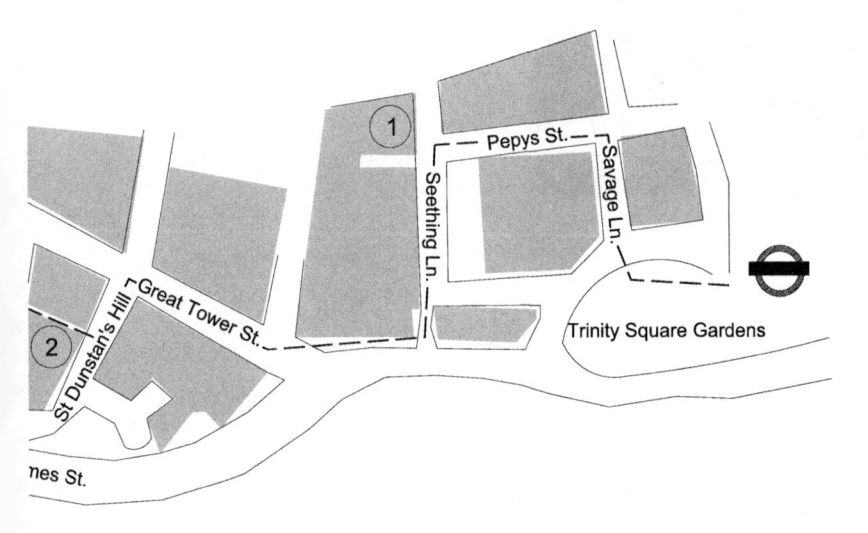

THE ROUTE

On this walk, we start with a medieval church which managed to survive the Great Fire. This enables us to see the architectural style that Wren reacted against so we can better understand the revolution that his churches represent.

We start at Tower Hill Station and walk into Trinity Square. Walk across the square and bear right at the corner along Savage Gardens and then left along Pepys Street. In front of you is our first stop: St. Olave's. This is the medieval church that we are going to use as the comparator for Wren's churches.

Stop 1. St Olave's

St Olave's is a beautiful medieval church, most famous for being Pepys' parish church, which we visit on the Samuel Pepys walk. It was spared the Great Fire and gives us a good understanding of what a medieval church looked like 400 years ago. Outside, it is clear that it has been added to, patched up and altered over the years. It is not symmetrical, logical or designed by a single hand. The church seems to have evolved over the years.

Inside, the immediate impression is of age, mystery and religiosity. It is dark with the altar at its eastern end. Aisles split the body of the church into three, obscuring the sightlines. The walls are richly decorated with monuments to the dead, including those to Samuel Pepys and his wife, and the windows are full of stained glass. This is a place of mysticism.

Exit the church, walk down Seething Lane, turn right and then cross busy Great Tower Street.

Walk along Great Tower Street and turn first left down St Dunstan's Hill. On your right you come across one of the most beautiful and romantic gardens in the city. It houses the remains of our second church.

Stop 2. St Dunstan in the East

Once one of the richest churches in the city it was damaged by the Great Fire but not destroyed. Wren rebuilt the tower and repaired the body of the church. It was significantly rebuilt in 1820 as a very early example of the Gothic Revival which swept Victorian society and led to the building of the Houses of Parliament and St Pancras Station amongst many others. The church was very badly damaged in the war and it was left as a monument to the suffering of the city. It's now often used for fashion or wedding photos.

Come out at the opposite side of the church into Idol Lane and follow it into St Dunstan's Lane. Turn right into St. Mary at Hill. On your left you'll see a narrow entrance proclaiming 'To the Church'. Go through to the hidden churchyard of St Mary at Hill. Have a look at the church wall across the old graveyard. Great windows, uncluttered by stained glass, let in the maximum amount of light into the church.

We will be returning to St. Mary in a few minutes. Continue walking up the hill and opposite you, across Eastcheap, you'll see our next church.

Stop 3. St Margaret Pattens

This is a very beautiful Wren church with the third tallest steeple in the city. Its curious name is due to the patten makers who lived in Rood Lane running by the church. A patten is a tall wooden clog that medieval Londoners used to don to keep them out of the filth in the alleys. Inside the church there is an exhibition detailing all you need to know (and perhaps a little more) about pattens. Inside, the church is relatively plain but with some fine furnishings. One in particular should be pointed out. At the west end of the church are two imposing churchwardens' pews. These are the only examples in the city of this type. Look carefully at the left hand pew and you can see the initials CW with the date 1686 carved in the ceiling. Some believe this is the great architect signing off his work, but equally the initials could stand for Church Warden. There is much of interest in the furniture of the church, including the coat of arms of James II (an unpopular choice given James's Catholic sympathies), an hour glass holder near the pulpit for timing sermons and hooks for hanging up parishioners' wigs. They're separated by a good few feet to deter fleas from jumping from one to the next.

Walk a little further down Eastcheap and take the first left down Lovat Lane. This is a beautiful little alley which conjures up images of its medieval origins. Half way down you come to the main entrance of St. Mary at Hill.

Stop 4. St Mary at Hill

This is the church whose churchyard we saw a few minutes ago: St Mary at Hill. This ancient church dates to at least the 12th century but may be considerably older. Today it's beautiful though bare as a devastating fire in 1988 destroyed its furnishings. This has the benefit of revealing just how revolutionary Wren's designs could be. The church is almost square and has a shallow dome at its centre. The impression is of lightness and clarity. We'll see other examples of Wren's work later but this really highlights the revolutionary break that Wren made with older medieval or Tudor styles of architecture. On your way out you can see in the entrance a stone carving of the last judgement.

Walk down Lovat Lane and turn right almost opposite Billingsgate Market. Soon you come to another Wren church: St Magnus the Martyr.

Stop 5. St Magnus the Martyr

This church is one of the most interesting in London. It was one of the first churches to be destroyed in the Great Fire and one of the first to be rebuilt by Wren. The fire is commemorated as the church houses a 17th century fire engine. One glance will show how ineffective it would have been once the fire had taken hold. There is also a remarkable — you may think slightly odd — statue of St Magnus, horned helmet, axe et al. It's very warlike given that he was supposed to be a peace-loving ruler of the Orkneys. More interesting or at least more historically accurate is a large model of the old, medieval London Bridge full of detail, even including the heads of traitors impaled on the southern entrance.

Much of the interior, including the statue of Magnus, the other statues and the stained glass windows, dates from the 1920's and it is very much part of the 'High

Church' tradition in the Church of England. We can be pretty sure that Wren would not have approved.

Outside is as interesting as the interior. The portico outside the church used to be the Toll House for London Bridge. This was erected in the 18th century and meant that part of the church had to be demolished to make way for it. Now, the tower of the church has been almost separated from its body with a passageway running under it. The windows facing onto the road have been blocked off in order to cut down the noise that once emanated from Billingsgate. Look also for a piece of iron-hard wood dating back to Roman times which is thought to be part of the old embankments for the Roman port.

Leave the church and cross the road, going up Fish Street Hill. In a hundred yards or so you suddenly see our next stop.

Stop 6. The Monument

The Monument was built to commemorate the Great Fire of London in 1666 which led to all the churches that we have been visiting. But it's also a monument to Wren's other interests as a scientist. The structure doubled as a scientific laboratory. He and another great scientist, Robert Hooke, designed the shaft for a telescope to observe the heavens and to investigate the movements of pendulums. In fact, there is still an underground space for a laboratory beneath the ticket office. However, it was never successful as vibrations from the heavy carts using nearby roads interfered with the experiments. It remains, however, a monument to Wren's importance as a polymath and his role within the scientific revolution of the late 17th century. As you leave, take a glance at the great carving on the Monument's west side where the rebuilding of London is portrayed. It shows, amongst much else, Charles II with the plans for London with builders busily reconstructing the city on the top right corner.

Walk away from the Monument to cross King William Street and then walk left down Cannon Street. Turn right up Abchurch Lane and very soon you come across an open space which once was the churchyard of St Mary Abchurch.

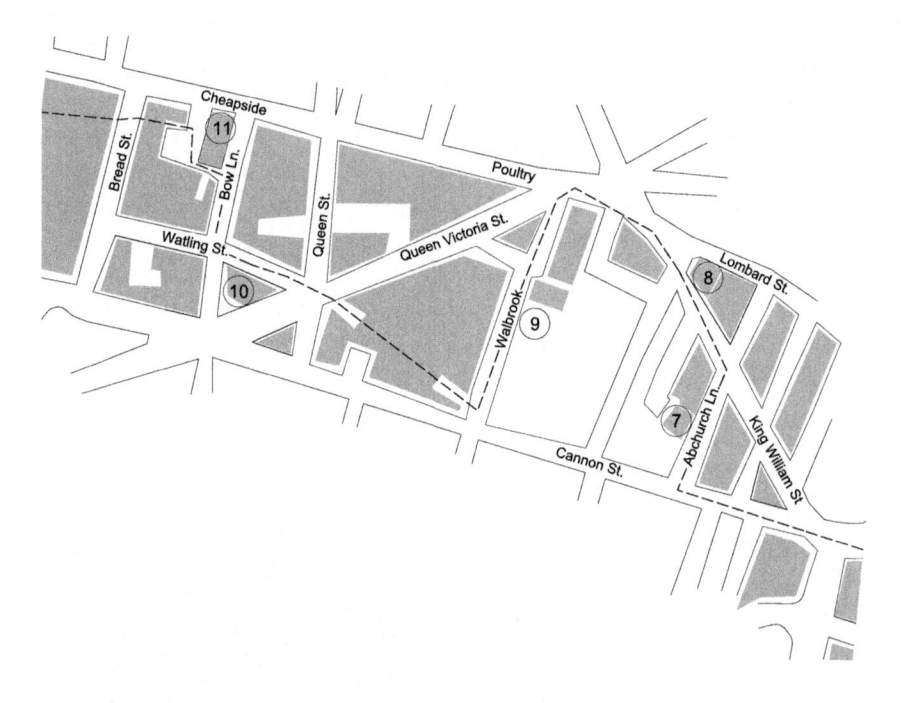

7. **St Mary Abchurch**

8. **St Mary Woolnoth**

9. **St Stephen's Walbrook**

10. **St Mary Aldermary**

11. **St Mary le Bow**

Stop 7. St Mary Abchurch

This church is a lovely example of Wren's more homely work and has been spared both the Blitz and the Victorians' exuberant improvements. It's probably the least altered of all of the churches that we visit. It contains a fine reredos by Grinling Gibbons, the only known example in the city, as well as sword rests given by various Lord Mayors of London.

Walk round the church and then turn left along King William Street. At its junction with Lombard Street stands the extraordinary church of St. Mary Woolnoth.

Stop 8. St Mary Woolnoth

This is not a Wren church but was designed by his apprentice, Nicholas Hawksmoor. Looking at the outside it's pretty obvious that this is something very different from most of Wren's churches. The building appears squat, strong and almost fortress-like with turrets, rather than spires, scowling down on Bank Station. One architectural critic has argued that Wren's churches point towards the heavens while Hawksmoor's are rooted in the earth. This is certainly true of this church.

The interior is more graceful, lighter and airier than you would expect. It's also full of history. At the end of the 18th century, the church was at the centre of the movement to abolish the slave trade. This was thanks to its remarkable rector, John Newton, who had been a captain of slave ships but had then repented and published a book attacking the trade. He was a friend and spiritual adviser to William Wilberforce and had time to write some of the most popular hymns in the English language, including *Amazing Grace*.

Continue along King William Street, bearing left past Mansion House, and then left down Walbrook to St Stephen's.

Stop 9. St Stephen's Walbrook

This church is regarded by many as one of the great masterpieces of Wren's work. Outside, it looks odd to say the least, and its appearance is not enhanced by the sacrilege to both God and coffee with a Starbucks tacked on the side. But once you step inside, the sensation is breath-taking. It is full of light with the altar (carved by Henry Moore) right in the centre of the church. Another fine reredos is at the east end of the church. Above you, there is a beautiful dome which, it is thought, was a prototype for St. Paul's.

Walk a few more steps along Walbrook, then turn right through the Bloomberg Arcade. Take a left and cross Queen Victoria Street and enter pedestrianised Watling Street opposite. Watling Street is of course the old Roman road which runs from Dover to Anglesey. Our little bit once linked London Bridge to St Paul's. On your left, there is a statue of a cordwainer, or shoe maker. The name is a corruption of Cordoba in Spain, where the finest medieval leather came from. The statue stands outside what is perhaps Wren's most 'Gothic' church: St Mary Aldermary.

Stop 10. St Mary Aldermary

This is so different from St Stephen's. It is a much more medieval-looking church and a good example of the perpendicular style. No one knows quite why Wren designed this the way he did. Perhaps the congregation had specified that it should resemble the destroyed church and he went along with their wishes. Its shape, certainly, is medieval. Look at the wall behind the altar. It's very much askew from the body of the church. This is because it's been built to accommodate an ancient alley running along the back; an example of how Wren had to squeeze his buildings into ancient sites. The most striking feature of the church, however, is above you. The ceiling is gorgeous and reminds us of the fan-vaulting of earlier times. However, this is not stone but plaster work and it gives the church a lightness at odds with its medieval character.

Leave the church and carry on along Watling Street. In front of us is the looming mass of St. Paul's, but we take a swift diversion. First, turn right down Bow Lane where at its corner there's a pub, Ye Olde Watling, which may have been built by Wren to house the workers building St Paul's. Its website claims that the plans for St Paul's were drawn up in its dining room. As you reach the end of Bow Lane there is an alley on your left which takes you into Bow Churchyard with, on your right, the church of St. Mary le Bow.

Stop 11. St Mary le Bow

This is perhaps the most important parish church that we visit, and certainly one of the oldest. It was called le Bow probably after the bow shaped windows that the Normans introduced into Anglo-Saxon London after 1066. The crypt claims to be the oldest continually used room in London as it hosts the Archbishop of Canterbury's meetings where new bishops swear their allegiance. The church also houses the Bow bells and, according to legend, if you're born within their sound you can claim to be a cockney. The reason for that is that 'cockney' was originally used to describe all Londoners and the Bow bells used to ring out the curfew for the city during medieval times.

Unfortunately, the church was badly damaged during the Blitz but has been sympathetically restored following Wren's original designs. It's open, airy and based on a square, allowing all to access services. Underneath, there is the hidden treasure of an extensive crypt with features going back to Roman times. It now houses a restaurant and a chapel and is a good place to stop for a coffee half-way through the walk.

Come out of the church, walk past the statue of Captain John Smith of Pocahontas fame and through the alley way that leads through the modern shopping centre of 1 New Change. In front of you is Wren's masterpiece, St. Paul's Cathedral. Walk to your left around the cathedral.

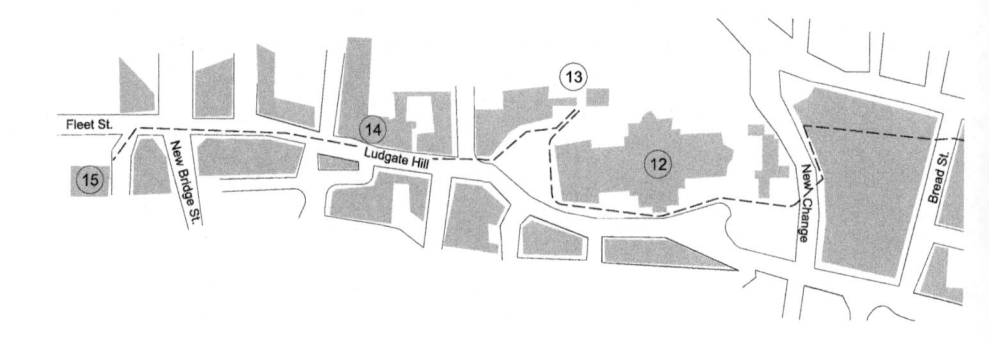

12. **St Paul's Cathedral**

13. **Temple Bar**

14. **St Martin within Ludgate**

15. **St. Brides**

Stop 12. St Paul's Cathedral

The exterior is awe-inspiring in its scale and the richness of its decoration. As you walk round, look up, and just underneath the dome you should be able to see a carved Phoenix rising from the flames and the word Resurgam (I will rise again) commemorating the rebuilding of London and its cathedral.

To go inside carries a hefty admission fee but it is worth a visit as it is one of the very greatest buildings in London. It has also been the site of many of Britain's great state occasions as well as the final resting place of its heroes. Nelson and Wellington both lie here, the former in a sarcophagus designed for Cardinal Wolsey in the 1520's. To do it justice you will need to arm yourself with a dedicated guidebook as there is so much to see. The cathedral is seen as Wren's masterpiece and it is fitting that he is buried here.

Keep walking round the front steps of the cathedral and in front of you leading into Paternoster Square is our next stop.

Stop 13. Temple Bar

Temple Bar used to stand where Fleet Street turns into Strand and marked the western boundary of the city. The imposing gatehouse you see before you was taken down in the 1760s and then spent 200 years in a stately home in the country. Returned to London, it forms an impressive entrance to Paternoster Square. The gate was designed by Wren and was meant to glorify the Stuart dynasty. The statue on the left is Charles I while his son Charles II is on the right. On the reverse of the gate is James II. Wren's efforts to enhance the reputation of the Stuarts wasn't particularly successful: James was thrown out after only 4 years during the so-called Glorious Revolution. But Temple Bar reminds us that Wren wasn't just a church architect but was involved in dozens of projects of all kinds throughout London and beyond.

Retrace your steps and start walking down Ludgate Hill. On your right, in a few hundred yards is our next church.

Stop 14. St Martin within Ludgate

This is one of the least altered Wren churches and is a part of the famous view looking up towards the dome of St Paul's from Fleet Street. It was built just inside the city walls, hence its name being: within Ludgate. As you go inside, you pass through a large entrance hall designed to insulate the church from the noise of the carts struggling up Ludgate Hill. Its shape is almost square inside. Look out for the font which has a Greek palindrome inscribed upon it which roughly translates to *'Wash my sins, not just my face'*. There is also some fine woodwork around the doors, along with original pews. In Wren's time it would have been much lighter as it would not have the Victorian stained glass which now darkens the church.

Exit the church, keep walking down Ludgate Hill and cross Bridge Street to continue along Fleet Street. 50 yards on your left an opening leads you directly to our next and final church: St. Bride's.

Stop 15. St Bride's Fleet Street

This is, perhaps, the most famous Wren parish church and is immediately recognisable by its wonderful steeple, the model for countless wedding cakes and still the highest in the city. The church is extraordinarily historic. It's built on Roman foundations, was certainly there in Saxon times, rebuilt by the Normans and again in medieval times. Wren's rebuilding after the Fire of London was one of his most expensive projects but the interior was all but destroyed during the Blitz. It has been beautifully restored and it remains a wonderfully impressive church. Look out for the trompe-l'oeil behind the altar.

Perhaps the true glory of the church lies beneath, in the crypt. There is a treasure trove beneath the church including a Roman pavement. There are exhibits spanning two thousand years of St Bride's history as well as an exhibition dedicated to the church's links to Fleet Street. It also hosts an annual lecture on Christopher Wren as well as concerts and recitals.

This is a very fitting place to end our walk through Wren's legacy.

AND FINALLY

The closest stations are Blackfriars, Farringdon, City Thameslink or St. Paul's.

There are many wonderful pubs along Fleet Street. The standout is the atmospheric Ye Olde Cheshire Cheese, a little further down Fleet Street, which has a literary history going back 300 years. But perhaps the best one to visit is the Old Bell. It's right next to St Brides and overlooks the churchyard. Crucially, it claims to have been built by Christopher Wren to house the workers building St Paul's. What more can you ask for?

FURTHER EXCURSIONS

To see more of Wren's work, the obvious place to start is Greenwich where he produced one of the great urban complexes including, of course, the Royal Observatory. My *Walking London's History* has a walk and chapter on Greenwich. You could also go to Chelsea Hospital or Kensington Palace, both of which he designed.

4. ALEXANDER POPE AND THE ARCADIAN THAMES

In this chapter, we are going to rediscover the aristocratic life of early 18th century England by taking perhaps the most beautiful walk in London, along the banks of the Thames from Richmond to Twickenham. In particular, we'll be walking with Alexander Pope (1688-1744), the preeminent poet of his day. He was certainly no aristocrat. In fact, he started life with very few advantages. His parents were linen merchants and he was born in Lombard Street in the centre of the city. They were Catholics and so were subject to the harsh anti-Catholic laws of the time. These prevented Catholics from going to university, serving in the professions or the army or becoming an MP. Indeed, the Pope family had to leave London as they weren't allowed to live within 10 miles of its centre. As a result, his schooling was interrupted and rudimentary, coming to an end at the age of 12. He also had terrible health problems with tuberculosis of the spine leading to a hunched back and he grew to only 4' 6". A friend wrote that he had *'a poor, crazy, deformed body,' 'a mere Pandora's box containing all the physical ills that ever afflicted humanity'*.

Despite these obstacles he was a precocious scholar. By the age of 21, Pope had already made his name as a significant poet with the publication of the Pastoral Poems. He went on to make his fortune in his twenties by retranslating Homer's Iliad. He was suddenly a rich man and with the proceeds of the Iliad, he built a house in the riverside village of Twickenham in 1719. He lived in this house for the rest of his life and, when he died, he was buried in Twickenham's parish church.

Today, Pope is largely forgotten in popular culture with his poems being very much of their age. However, we use his phrases all the time. He has more entries than anyone, bar Shakespeare, in the Oxford Dictionary of Quotations. They include *'To damn with faint praise'*, *'Eternal sunshine of the spotless mind'*, *'A little learning is a dangerous thing'*, *'Hope springs eternal'*, *'Fools rush in where angels fear to tread'* and, perhaps most important, *'To err is human, to forgive, divine.'*

By the 1720's, Pope was the leading poet of the age, and through his essays and letters he was introducing a new sensibility of art, beauty and nature into the nation's culture. Heavily reliant on imagery derived from ancient Greece, it emphasised a new aesthetic of beauty within nature. The formalism which underpinned the Tudor and Stuart gardens was swept away and in its place was an emphasis on nature in which man could flourish. In garden design gave rise to what became known as the English Landscape Movement which spread across the western world. The boundaries between art, nature and landscape were blurred. The aim was to find beauty in the landscape and natural world and, where necessary, to enhance it. This thinking was to inspire the work of the great garden designers of the 18th century such as Capability Brown and William Kent and can be seen in dozens of stately homes across England. Pope was at the centre of this movement. In his Epistle to Lord Burlington, for instance, he wrote *'Let all in nature not be forgot, but treat the goddess like a modest fair; Nor overdressed, nor leave her wholly bare.'*

Pope not only wrote about nature and beauty but put his ideals into practice, designing his own and others' gardens to fit in with this aesthetic. It was this cultural movement that inspired the term *'the Arcadian Thames'*. Arcadia refers to an area in Ancient Greece which symbolised a rural paradise, where life was simpler and more bucolic than the crowded city. It was a place where humanity could co-exist in harmony with nature. The term began to be applied, in particular, to the stretch of river between Hampton Court and Chiswick. The Thames' beauty here had long been recognised, and with easy access to the Court in Westminster, monarchs and nobles had for centuries built their summer homes along its banks. Edward I had often stayed at the manor house in Sheen, Henry VII had had it rebuilt as Richmond Palace, Henry VIII enjoyed Hampton Court and the Georgian kings stayed at Kew.

In our period though, a second alternative court was beginning to appear between Twickenham and Richmond. This was based not so much on 'noble' birth but on wit and intellect. At its heart was a remarkable woman: Henrietta Howard, Countess of Suffolk. She had been orphaned at 12 and married into the aristocracy but her husband was a violent, unfaithful drunk. She was forced to live in squalor and poverty but finally managed to gain a position as Lady of the Bedchamber to Queen Caroline, wife of George II. Her position was further enhanced when she became the King's mistress, a position tolerated by the Queen. When the relationship came to an end after more than 10 years, the King gave Henrietta a significant sum of money and she used it to build a beautiful house on the Thames: Marble Hill.

Around Henrietta congregated some of the greatest writers, wits and poets of the time. These included Jonathan Swift of Gulliver's Travels fame, John Gay who wrote the Beggar's Opera and, later, Horace Walpole, son of the first British Prime Minister, and the man who launched the neo-gothic revival in Britain, both through his writings and the architecture for his house at Strawberry Hill. Alexander Pope was one of Henrietta's closest friends. He helped her design the gardens and was a constant visitor to her home at Marble Hill. There the conversation was witty and often acerbic about life in the royal palaces, scandals in Parliament and the latest artistic fashions in London. Poking fun could be dangerous and Pope made many enemies which meant that for some years he carried loaded pistols in his pockets.

After Henrietta's death in 1767, Marble Hill continued to be used occasionally by the Royal Family: the Prince Regent, the future George IV, used it to house his mistress, Maria Fitzherbert in the 1790s. Architecturally, the house was very significant, many critics seeing it as an almost perfect example of the Palladian style in England. It was famous and became the blueprint for many stately houses both in England and the American Colonies of the time.

Marble Hill was only one of a number of houses along this stretch of the Thames. There had been a few before Henrietta's but the heyday of the area was from around 1720 to 1760 when aristocrats, merchants and artists built several fine homes there. The attractions of Twickenham and Richmond have endured from then till today. Artists and writers, such as J M W Turner, Virginia Woolf and Noel Coward, once lived there. At the time of writing, national treasures, Brian Blessed, David Attenborough and Richard E Grant have homes in the area.

FURTHER READING

A book I found good on the Twickenham 'court' of the 18th century:

King's Mistress, Queen's Servant, by Tracy Borman

THE WALK

This walk is one of the most beautiful in London at any time of the year but especially so in spring and early summer. It takes us down the banks of the Thames at its most bucolic but there's also much of historic interest along the way. We visit three great houses from the 17th and 18th centuries, and if you have the energy, there are a few more to see. While we will be concentrating on the first half of the 18th century, there's lots to see from closer to our own times. We'll be seeing where rock royalty burst onto the scene in the sixties, and there could also be a little bit of rugby.

1. Richmond Palace
2. Virginia Woolf Statue
3. Bernardo O'Higgins Statue
4. Richmond Bridge
5. Belgian Village
6. Marble Hill House
7. Orleans House
8. Thomas Twining's House
9. St Mary's Church
10. Eel Pie Island
11. Ladies Statue
12. York House

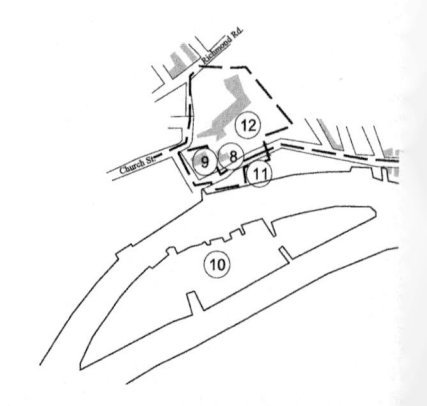

4. Alexander Pope and the Arcadian Thames 57

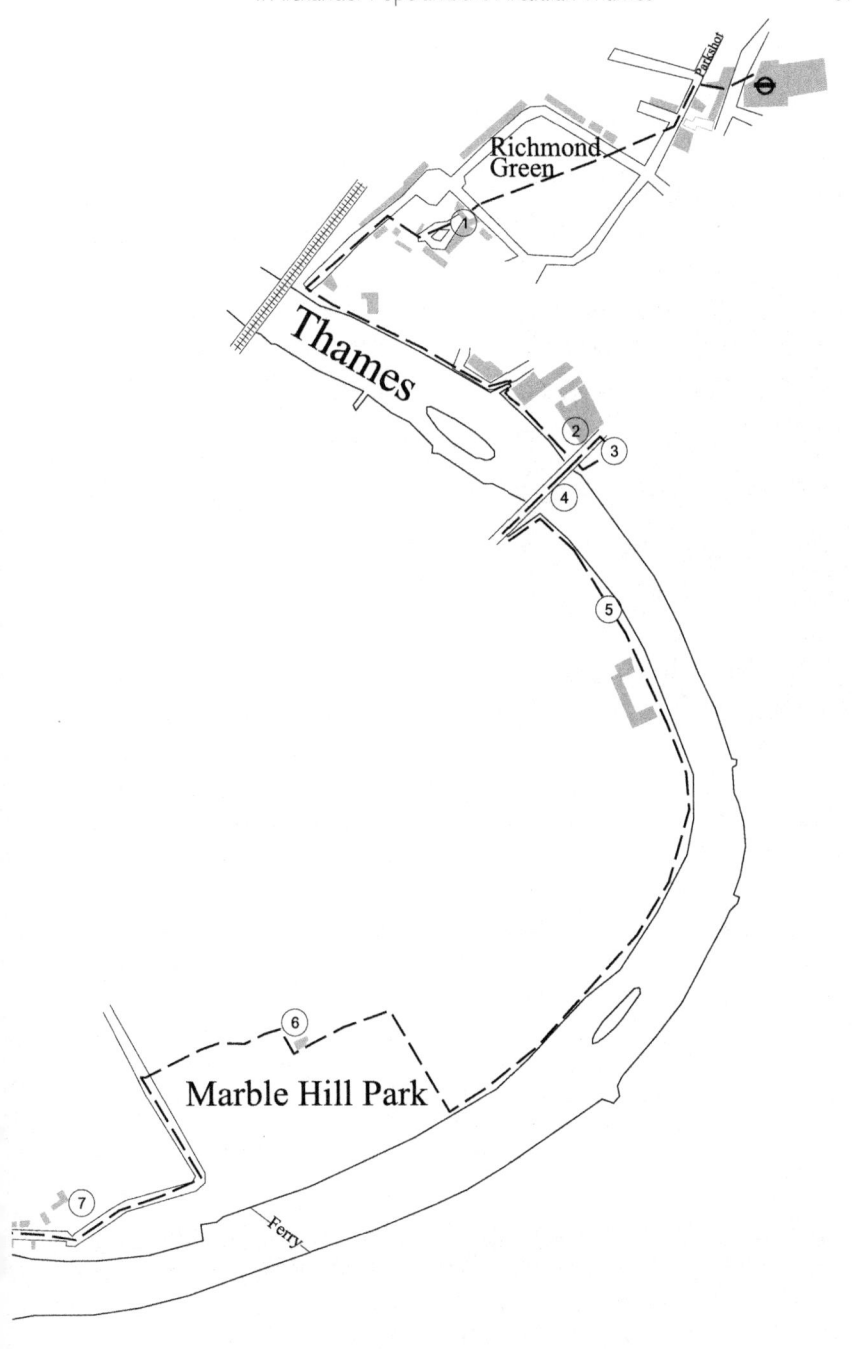

THE ROUTE

Stop 1

You arrive at the gatehouse to the old Richmond Palace. Royal connections go back over 700 years to 1299 when Edward I brought his court to what was then called Sheen. Nearly 100 years later, Richard II made it his main royal palace. You can see why; it's in a great location, perched on a broad terrace overlooking the Thames. The gatehouse to the palace you're looking at was rebuilt in 1498 by Henry VII and he changed its name from Sheen to Richmond after his family seat of Richmond in Yorkshire. The Palace became a favoured summer retreat of the Tudors and its residents included Catherine of Aragon, Ann of Cleves and Mary I. Elizabeth I liked to stay here often and it was the palace in which she died.

Walk through the gatehouse in front of you, noting the fine Tudor architecture on your left, but bear down the little street to your right, and then turn left into Old Palace Lane. This is full of little workers' cottages — today very much out of the price range of ordinary workers. When you reach the riverside, turn to your left and walk towards the stone bridge. In the river opposite you, you'll see three islands. The largest one used to house a summer palace built by Richard II for his Queen, Anne of Bohemia.

Continue to walk along the river towards the bridge. On your left there is a broad terrace with benches overlooking the river.

Stop 2

On the top terrace, at its far end, is a bench with a statue of a woman sitting on it. This is of Virginia Woolf who lived in Richmond for 10 years before moving back to Bloomsbury. She came here to recuperate after suffering a nervous collapse just after her marriage to Leonard Woolf. He nursed her back to health and between them they set up Hogarth Press as a distraction. It later became one of the most famous publishing houses in the world, with writers like T S Elliot amongst its authors. If you're a fan, you will want to pay homage and sit a while with her.

Carry on walking under the bridge and then immediately turn left up a flight of stairs.

Stop 3
As you walk up you'll see a bust in front of you; this is of the liberator and founding father of the Republic of Chile with one of the great names in history: Bernardo O'Higgins. He spent some time in Richmond as a schoolboy and was influenced by the ideas of the other South American liberators living in London. He went back to South America where he led the fight for Chilean independence from Spain.

Walk on to the bridge and cross the river.

Stop 4
Stop on Richmond Bridge and admire the beautiful view upstream. JMW Turner painted both the bridge and the view. It is the bucolic Thames at its best and from here you can easily see why it could be compared to Arcadia.

Before you reach the end of the bridge, steps lead down to a slip into the river. Go down the stairs to gain the towpath, along which we now start walking.

Stop 5
After a few hundred yards, you come across a small square with two very different stories to tell. This was the site of the 'Belgian Village' on the Thames where thousands of refugees lived after their country was invaded by the Germans at the outbreak of the First World War. They set up an armaments factory here along

with a sizable community. After the War, it hosted an ice skating rink which, at the time, was the biggest in the world.

Keep walking along the towpath until you reach the architectural highlight of our walk; Marble Hill House.

Stop 6

The house is just about perfect. It was commissioned by Henrietta Howard and built by a young architect, Robert Morris. It was greatly admired at the time. A Georgian guide book to the area claimed *'Among all the villas of this neighbourhood, Lady Suffolk's, which we sail past on the left, makes the best appearance from the river.'* It still does today.

Walk up the right hand side of the house to visit the newly refurbished Grotto. This was designed by Pope and his friends for Henrietta. It gives us an opportunity to imagine the much more famous 'Pope's Grotto', a mile or so up river. If the house is open, it's well worth a visit to see an elegant early Georgian interior and there's a good café if you need refreshments. Details of opening times etc. are at **www.english-heritage.org.uk**

If you wish, you could make a detour to JMW Turner's House which is at 40 Sandycombe Road, around 500 yards away. The great painter designed and had it built in 1813 and used it both to house his father and as a summer retreat for the next dozen years. If you do want to visit, you'll find opening times etc. at **www.turnershouse.org**. It is quite a modest house but interesting if you're interested in Turner. The fact that Turner lived here shows that Twickenham was still attracting artists and the intelligentsia 100 years after our period.

Rejoin the riverbank and across the river you'll see a very different grand house. This is not Georgian but Jacobean. It's Ham House, built in 1610, over 100 years before Marble Hill. It was owned by a friend and courtier of Charles I, William Murray, and it stayed in his family for over 300 years. Today, it's a National Trust property. You could make a diversion to Ham House, although a visit demands at least 2 hours or more. If you fancy the trip, you can take a Hammerton ferry from just by Marble Hill House. This only costs £1 and takes you across the river to Ham

House in a couple of minutes. Details are at **www.hammertonsferry.com**. It's worth remembering the ferry if you want to do a circular walk and return to Richmond.

Otherwise keep walking along the bank for a few hundred yards until a wall forces you away from the river. In front of you is our next great mansion: Orleans House. Walk in through the gates.

Stop 7

Orleans House was built in 1710 for James Johnson, an early Georgian Politician. Its name derives from Louis Phillippe, Duc d'Orleans, the future King of France. He lived here in exile from 1815-17 and his son also lived here in the 1850s and 1860s. Much of the house has gone, but what has been saved is the extraordinary octagonal room. This was built in 1720 and has been spectacularly refurbished in white and gold. It has hosted visits by George I, George II and Queen Victoria. The house also hosts a good café and an excellent art gallery. For details see **www.orleanshousegallery.org**

Once you've had your fill of Orleans House, continue along the walled road between the house and the river bank. You soon come to some suburban houses and then to a wonderful pub overlooking the river: the White Swan. This is a lovely place with a patio on the river bank. The only slight problem is that at high tide you may get marooned there. Helpfully, the pub provides the times of the tides and used to have wellington boots for stranded drinkers.

Carry on along the road until you see the back of St Mary's, the parish church.

Stop 8

Just before you get there, the fine house on your right – with an imposing sun dial – was built and owned by Thomas Twining, the tea importer and merchant. He made a fortune from the fashionable, but very expensive, beverage and he used the proceeds to build this fine house.

Walk right round the back of the church and shortly you'll see two plaques.

Stop 9

The first is to Thomas Twining, erected by his children *'to the memory of a most indulgent and worthy parent'*. The next is to the memory of Mary Beach who was Alexander Pope's nurse and servant. She looked after him for 38 years and Pope erected the plaque to her *'in gratitude to a faithful old servant'*. The church itself dates back to 1714, although its tower is 300 years older. Inside it is beautiful, but unfortunately not often open. If you can get inside, look for the memorial to Alexander Pope who is buried there under a stone slab, marked simply P. There is also a plaque to him on the wall.

Walk round the church and exit right down some steps towards the Thames and make your way to the riverbank by another pub, the Barmy Arms.

Stop 10

You are now directly opposite the famous Eel Pie Island; one of the great cultural hotspots of the sixties. In the 1960's this was the birthplace of British R&B where a succession of great bands burst on to the burgeoning music scene. The Rolling Stones, David Bowie, The Moody Blues, Pink Floyd, The Yardbirds, Black Sabbath, Led Zeppelin and The Who all played at the Eel Pie Island Hotel, a crumbling ruin of a Victorian tea room. By 1970, it had become the largest hippie commune in the UK; a place of great ill-repute. The hotel mysteriously and conveniently burnt down in 1971. The commune was dispersed and the site was then redeveloped as a boatyard. You can get on to the island; you'll see a footbridge leading to the island 50 yards upstream. However, the trip can't really be recommended as you enter an alley running between private workshops and houses. There's little to see but, at least, you could say 'I was there' even if you're 60 years too late to catch the music.

We, however, are turning to our left away from the bridge and into a small park overlooking the river called Champions Wharf. On its right there is a children's playground and to the left, Twickenham's memorial to Alexander Pope. It's a small area with a long semi-circular bench which is engraved with some of his most famous sayings. It's a lovely spot to sit for a bit. Just by the river there is a gate which we pass through along a short riverside path with great views towards Richmond. After 20 yards or so, a gap in the hedge leads to our next stop.

Stop 11
You're standing in front of the Naked Ladies, a group of Italian marble statues. They were probably carved at the beginning of the 19th century out of Carrara marble and were installed here a hundred years later by the gardens' owner, Sir Ratan Tata. (think Tata Steel). They are an extraordinary and unexpected sight as they cavort among the fountains. We walk away from the statues towards a formal pond and then turn left over an ornamental footbridge to our last great house.

Stop 12
This is York House, a fine Jacobean mansion, built in the 1630's for a courtier of Charles I. It passed through various hands including Philippe, Comte de Paris, the Orleans pretender to the French throne (which by then had been abolished). Today it has a more mundane existence as the municipal offices of Richmond upon Thames Council. As you move to the right round the house you can see its beautiful gardens. Walking past tennis courts, you come out on to Richmond Road almost opposite the Eel Pie Island Museum. We walk down the path on our left towards the church but follow Church Street into what used to be the old Twickenham High Street.

Which is where our walk ends facing a plethora of pubs, cafés and little specialist shops.

AND FINALLY

There are lots of fine pubs in Twickenham. You could walk back to the Barmy Arms or White Swan if you fancy a drink by the river. My favourite pub, though, is the Eel

Pie Hotel in Church Street which is welcoming, has got decent food and beer and its back room has ephemera dating back to the heyday of the Island.

To get home you could walk back along the river to Richmond, using the Hammerton ferry to walk along the opposite bank and get the classic view of Marble Hill House from across the river. If not, you can get a bus down Richmond Road to get back to our start point, or Twickenham Station is 400 yards to your north.

FURTHER EXCURSIONS

There is more to see in Twickenham if you're interested in Pope and 18th century life. To visit the site of Pope's Twickenham House, walk along the main road, King Street, bear left down Cross Deep and after around 800 yards you come to Radnor House, a private school. In its gardens lies the famous Grotto built by Alexander Pope. At the time of writing, it's being refurbished and when completed the Trust hope to have it open to the public around 30 times a year. To find out when it's open see **www.popesgrotto.org.uk**. Just across the road there is a plaque recording the entrance to Pope's Villa. Unfortunately, there is nothing of the house left.

There are, however, a couple of sights a little further on. You pass a fine riverside park with lovely views. Radnor Park has a gazebo and summer house dating from the 18th century and gives you another glimpse of what gracious Georgian living would be like.

Finally, if you walk up Waldegrave Road at the end of Radnor Park, you shortly come to the extraordinary Strawberry Hill House, home of novelist Horace Walpole. He was a close friend of Henrietta Howard and had it built in 1749 shortly after Pope had died. It is a fine sight and marked the start of the Georgian neo-gothic revival. You can check its opening times at **www.strawberryhillhouse.org.uk**.

To get back to Twickenham or Richmond from here jump on the 33 bus which will take you to both centres.

5. THE BRUNELS IN LONDON

In the 19th century, London changed out of all recognition. It expanded further and faster than at any time in its history. From a European capital with a million people in 1800 (and an area of perhaps 10 square miles), by the end of the century it was the greatest city on earth, with 8 million people and stretching over 300 square miles. This expansion was fuelled by London being at the very centre of the largest and richest empire the world had ever seen.

Driving this urban revolution were the great engineers of the 19th century, such as Bazalgette, Stephenson and Telford, but there is one name that stands out above them all: Brunel. The family produced three generations of great engineers. The founding father of the dynasty was Sir Marc Brunel. He was followed by his now more famous son, Isambard and Isambard's son, Henry, continued the family tradition. Between them they spanned the 19th century and, in their time, they transformed not just London but the modern world.

Let us start with the pater familias, Marc Brunel. He was not a Londoner but French, and in his early life was apprenticed into the Royal French Navy. While he was at sea, the French Revolution broke out and, on his return, Marc, an ardent royalist, was forced to flee into exile by the revolutionaries. He went to New York but not before meeting and falling in love with a young English governess, Sophie Kingdom. She was thrown into prison as a suspected English spy and daily expected the guillotine. Meanwhile, in America, Marc thrived, becoming Chief Engineer for the City of New York. But there were also opportunities back in London where Britain was at war with France. So Marc sailed for England. There he met up again with Sophie who had been released after the fall of Robespierre. They married and moved to Chelsea. He rapidly became both famous and wealthy designing equipment for the war effort. But in 1815, after the final defeat of Napoleon at the battle of Waterloo, peace broke out. And peace was not necessarily good for profits.

In 1821, Brunel was declared bankrupt and sent to a debtors' prison. With no sign of release, he began to correspond with the Russian Tsar about building bridges in St.

Petersburg. Alarmed at the prospect of losing one of their most eminent engineers, the Duke of Wellington, amongst others, started to press for his release. His debts were paid and he began work on the most revolutionary of his many projects: to build a tunnel under the Thames at Rotherhithe. This was a world-first. Nobody had dug a tunnel under a navigable river before, but as the city boomed and the streets and bridges became clogged, tunnels were needed. This was revolutionary work. Without the innovations that Marc Brunel introduced, it would be almost impossible to develop the mass transit systems on which cities now depend.

The tunnel at Rotherhithe took from 1825 to 1843 and cost the equivalent of millions of pounds in today's money. Marc introduced two truly innovative techniques into engineering practice. First, the caisson: a pre-fabricated tube to create the shaft of the tunnel, and, second, a rudimentary tunnelling machine where labourers, in a kind of giant honeycomb, cut inch by inch through the soil under the river. Both techniques, though much improved, are still used in tunnel construction today, which was why the Thames Tunnel is seen as so important in engineering history.

The work was extraordinarily dangerous. There were terrible floods where tunnellers were drowned underground. There were gas explosions and many men were made severely ill by the noxious conditions. But finally, it was finished and became one of the great tourist attractions of London. On its first day, some 50,000 people visited this wonder of the modern age. It was used as an underground ballroom, fairground and restaurant. But the project had run out of money and it closed before the approach roads could be built. For a decade it lay unused until an enterprising railway company used it to construct the first railway under the Thames. And it is still being used today almost 200 years on; a testament to the vision and skill of Marc Brunel.

Isambard, Marc's son and the most famous of the Brunel family, also worked on the Thames Tunnel. Indeed, at the age of 22, he was chief engineer on the project, directing the work of hundreds of men. He almost died there when a catastrophic flood killed the five other people working alongside him. He was badly injured but survived to launch a series of ground-breaking projects. Perhaps the most famous was the development of the Great Western Railway operating out of Paddington Station.

His work wasn't confined to railways. He built bridges, docks and ships. His greatest achievement was probably the ships. In Bristol he built the Great Western, at the time the longest ship in the world. He then built the Great Britain, seen as the first modern ship, as it was at the time the largest in the world with an iron hull and propeller drive. Finally, in 1852 Brunel built the Great Eastern in London. It was originally called the Leviathan and it's easy to see why; the ship was five times bigger than any ship ever built, 700 feet long, and completely dwarfing the Great Britain. It could carry 4,000 passengers or 10,000 soldiers to anywhere in the world. Its size was not surpassed for almost 60 years. It had 6 funnels, sails, paddle wheels and a propellor. It had luxurious cabins, but could carry enough coal to reach Australia and return home without refuelling. It was also revolutionary in its design. It had a double iron hull which made it far safer than other ships of the time. It was only after the Titanic disaster in 1913 that all ships had to adopt Brunel's innovation of 60 years before.

However, the project was marred by misfortune almost from the start. Its initial launch was unsuccessful. A winch broke and 2 labourers died. It took another 3 months before the great ship could be launched. On its maiden voyage a catastrophic explosion occurred which killed 5 sailors. It also indirectly killed Isambard. So bound up in this project was he that the stress of the explosion brought on a series of strokes which eventually killed him. He was only 53 and killed by overwork.

The ship continued, however. A failure at transporting people, it did end up transforming global communications. The telegraph had just been invented and to lay the necessary cables across the oceans you needed very large ships. For the next 20 years, the Great Eastern laid cables across the globe, revolutionising telecommunications. The time for messages to cross the Atlantic had gone *'From two weeks to two minutes'* as the advertising claimed. However, its cable-laying role eventually came to an end and the Great Eastern was finally broken up in Liverpool only 30 years after its launch. The only remaining part still on view is the Great Eastern's top mast which stands outside Liverpool FC's Anfield ground as its flagpole.

Isambard's son, Henry, also became a well-known engineer. He went into partnership with Sir John Wolfe Barry and designed with him docks and bridges. In particular, in London he designed the Blackfriars railway bridge which is still in use today and, most famously, they became chief engineers on Tower Bridge, one of the instantly recognised icons of London around the world.

So the Brunels transformed London, Britain and indeed the world. It's little wonder that in a BBC poll of 2002 to find the greatest Briton of all time that Isambard was voted no.2.

FURTHER READING

There are lots of books about Isambard. Perhaps the best is: *Brunel: The Man Who Changed the World,* by Steven Brindle.

THE WALK

This is not so much a walk as a river cruise and train journey through the heart of East London. It was one of the first walks I did when I took up guiding after retirement. I used to take a weekly walk for the Brunel Museum where we would end. It was devised by Robert Hulse, the then Director of the Museum and it remains one of my favourite excursions through London.

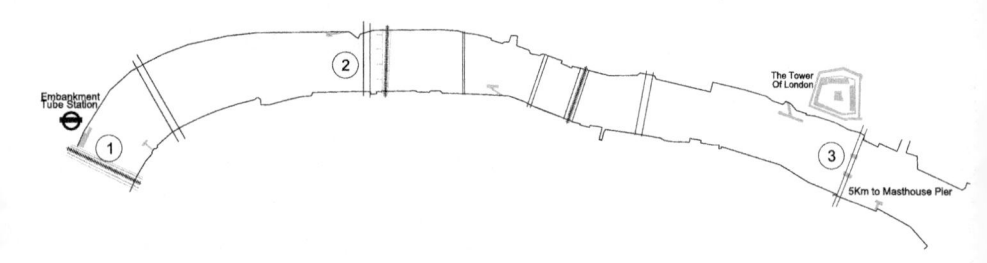

1. Hungerford Railway Bridge

2. Blackfriars Bridges

3. Tower Bridge

THE ROUTE

We start at Embankment Tube Station where, from the pier opposite, we take the boat to Masthouse Terrace on the Isle of Dogs.

Stop 1
As you get on the boat, take a look at Hungerford Railway Bridge in front of you. This is one of Isambard's first bridges. All that remains of it are the great red brick piers which hold up the railway into Charing Cross. Originally this was a road bridge taking produce into Hungerford Market which was later demolished to make way for the station. The original design was a beautiful suspension bridge. When it was dismantled, there was a public outcry as the railway bridge was so ugly. However, the chains were reused and they now support the Clifton Suspension Bridge in Bristol.

The boat takes you to Westminster before doing a U-turn and sailing downstream. This gives you a fine view of the piers again. What you may notice is that the northern pier is hard against the river bank while the southern is 100 yards or so into the river. Originally, the two piers were symmetrical; however, the building of the Embankment by Bazalgette extended the northern bank dramatically, thus narrowing the river.

Stop 2

As you cruise down river our next example of the Brunels' work comes at Blackfriars Bridge. There are in fact 3 bridges here, all very close to each other, and it can be a challenge to spot all the details.

The first is a road bridge. Look out for the beautiful engravings of birds at the top of the columns. You may notice that those facing downstream are seabirds, such as cormorants, while those facing upstream are freshwater birds, like swans.

The bridge achieved notoriety in 1982 when the body of Roberto Calvi was found hanging from the bridge. He was chairman of the Banco Ambrosiano with close links both to the Vatican and the Mafia. The bank had just collapsed and it's almost certain he was killed by the Mafia as punishment for losing their money and to prevent him from informing on them.

The second bridge, with its distinctive red columns, is an old railway bridge which took passengers from Kent into the City. It became too weak for modern trains but the remnants are listed so remain in place.

The third bridge is a Brunel bridge dating from 1885. It was designed by Henry Marc Brunel and his senior partner, John Wolfe Barry. It has proved to be a bit sturdier than the first railway bridge, serving commuters for almost 150 years.

We cruise on through the heart of the city with great views of St. Paul's on the north bank and Southwark Cathedral on the south.

Stop 3

We arrive at Tower Bridge. This too has a claim to be a Brunel Bridge, at least in part. John Wolfe Barry was the Chief Engineer and his partner was Henry Marc Brunel. The two of them worked together to design the lifting mechanisms of the bridge and when the Chief Architect died within a month of the building work starting, it left Wolfe and Brunel to complete the project.

Tower Bridge is one of the great engineering projects of the Victorian age and was at the cutting edge of the technology of the time. Today it is perhaps the iconic London building. At the time, though, reaction was much more mixed. The criticism levelled against it was that this symbol of progress and modernity had been dressed up in the clothes of the past; what should have been steel and steam had been turned into a medieval gatehouse.

We continue downstream. On both banks we'll see entrances to the great docks, old pubs dating back to the 16th century, and in front of us the glittering skyscrapers of Canary Wharf. We get off at Masthouse Terrace at the southernmost tip of the Isle of Dogs.

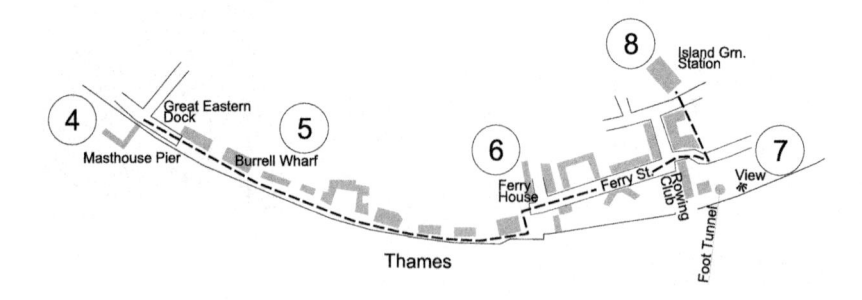

4. **Great Eastern**

5. **Burrell's Wharf**

6. **Ferry House Pub**

7. **View of Greenwich**

Stop 4

Walk up the pier and just to your right are all that remains of the site which saw the building of the greatest ship the world had even seen. This was possibly Isambard's most revolutionary project: the Great Eastern.

What you see now are the great chains (or at least their replicas) that pulled the ship into the river down wooden rollers. If the tide is low you can see that the ramp extends into the river. The first attempt at launching the great ship was a disaster. It was so big that to launch it normally, i.e. bow first would have been impossible as it was longer than the Thames is wide. So it had to be lowered into the water sideways, but a winch snapped and killed 2 of the workers. It was to take another 3 months before the ship was finally able to be floated off.

Today, it's difficult to envisage the scene of 170 years ago. The building works would have extended along the river bank and the noise would have been deafening with 30,000 iron plates and a million rivets being used. Today the riverside is much quieter and often almost deserted.

Continue walking downstream towards Greenwich.

Stop 5

On your left you come to Burrell's Wharf. In the first half of the 19th century, this area was devoted to iron works to serve the shipbuilding industry and this is where the plates and rivets for Brunel's great ship would have been manufactured. The buildings we see date from just after the construction of the Great Eastern.

Keep walking along the river bank until the path runs out and you're forced inland.

Stop 6

In front of you is the Ferry House, a pub dating back over 300 years. It used to service passengers on the horse ferry here and at low tide you can still see the remnants of the ferry on the shore line.

The view down East Ferry Road is almost like a time line of the history of the Isle of Dogs. You're standing on a raised embankment built more than 400 years ago to protect what was marshland from flooding. As you look down you can see successive styles of housing ranging from dockers' cottages to council housing of the 1930's to the glittering skyscrapers of Canary Wharf.

Walk right along Ferry Street noting the fine, old houses at the end of the road.

Stop 7

It's worthwhile to continue 100 yards past the rowing club into Island Gardens for one of the greatest views in London. You see Wren's Greenwich Palace and observatory from across the Thames. This was painted by, amongst others, Canaletto. His picture of the view is in the Queen's House which you see across the river in the centre of the view.

Retrace your steps and then walk to Island Gardens Station on the Docklands Light Railway.

Stop 8

We're going to take the train to Shadwell on one of the most spectacular train journeys in Britain. You need to take any train to Bank or Tower Gateway and the line winds over the remnants of the docks and past the great towers housing the world's financial institutions.

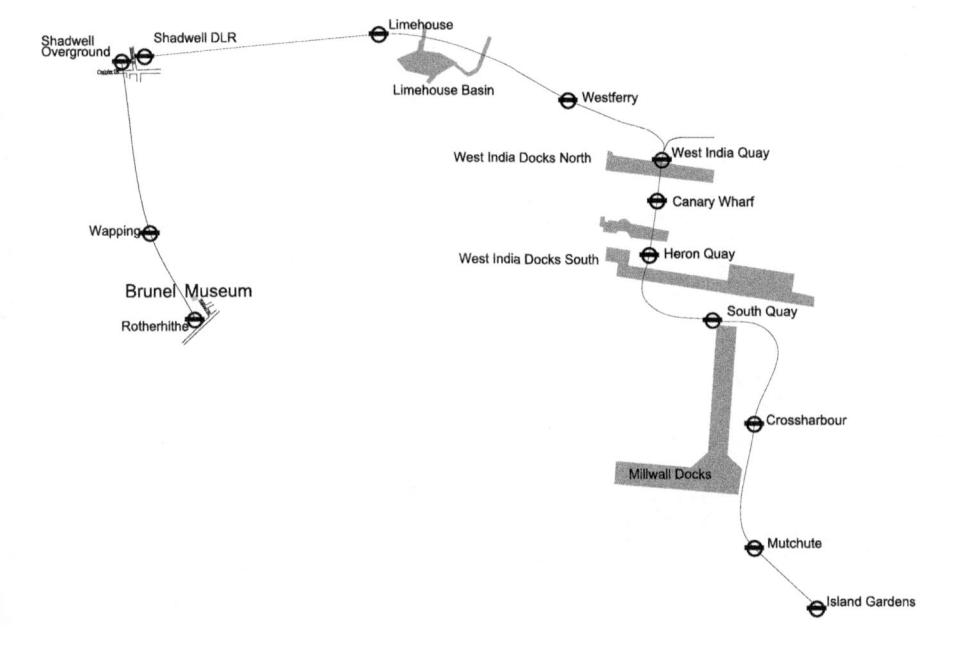

Along the way we pass:

- Mudchute, so called because this is where the mud excavated to build the docks was dumped. It's now an urban farm but during the war was the site of the anti-aircraft guns that tried to protect East London from the Blitz.
- The four great docks which made up the complex of the West India Docks.
- The buildings of Canary Wharf which started the regeneration of the Docklands.
- Just by Westferry station you can spy fine early 19th century houses built for the managers of the docks. They appear somewhat incongruous caught, as they are, between post war social housing and the financial tower blocks.
- Limehouse Basin which linked the docks with the national canal system.
- Cable Street, the scene in 1936 of clashes between Oswald Mosley's British Union of Fascists and the local community.

You get off at Shadwell DLR station. This is in the Parish of St. George's which for 200 years has been one of the most deprived neighbourhoods in London. Cross Watney Street and just to your left you'll see Shadwell Overground Station.

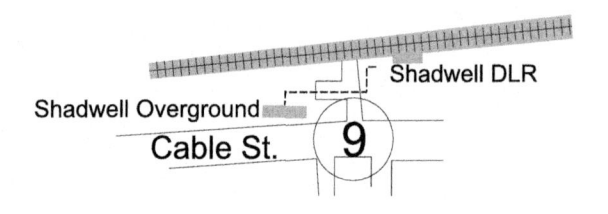

Descend and take any southbound train.

Stop 9

As we travel under the river, we'll be using the tunnel built by Marc Brunel nearly 200 hundred years ago. True aficionados of his work may want to get out at Wapping and look down the tunnel as the line descends under the river. It's the only place you can really see the actual tunnel. But do take great care, the platforms are very narrow and leaning over the tracks while a train approaches from behind is not a great idea.

Otherwise carry on till you reach Rotherhithe and get off the train.

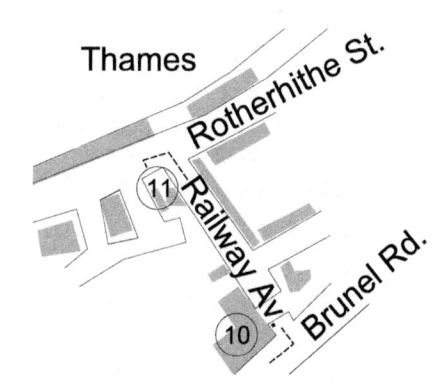

10. Rotherhithe Station

11. Brunel Museum

Stop 10

In Rotherhithe station there are 2 plaques at the bottom of the escalators commemorating the Tunnel and a very small display about the Brunels at the top.

Emerge from the station, turn left and immediately left again along Railway Avenue until on your left you reach the Brunel Museum.

Stop 11

The Brunel Museum is an unexpectedly beautiful place. Outside there is a courtyard surrounded by trees and with benches that recall some of Isambard's bridges. The museum itself falls into two parts, a small exhibition and then a visit to the shaft of the tunnel.

In the old engine house, there are exhibits about the building of the Thames Tunnel and the Great Eastern. Some of the exhibits are wonderful: Victorian souvenirs of the opening of the tunnel, a painting showing the world's first underwater banquet with the Duke of Wellington in attendance, as well as explanatory panels around the walls. See **www.thebrunelmuseum.com** for opening times.

Outside the museum is the shaft of the tunnel. You're able to descend 50 feet and see first hand the extraordinary innovation of Marc Brunel. You can see the chains that held the caisson together, the soot deposited by Victorian steam trains as they chugged through the tunnel from the 1860s onwards and feel the vibrations from the trains which still use the tunnel today. The shaft is often used as a space for concerts, plays and parties and can be a wonderfully atmospheric place. The top of the shaft is an urban garden where they grow the botanicals for the Midnight Apothecary where on summer evenings you can drink cocktails and eat toasted marshmallows around an open fire.

AND FINALLY

There's only one pub to go to and that's the Mayflower, built on the wharf from which the Mayflower sailed with the Pilgrim Fathers in 1620. It's wonderfully atmospheric with a jetty reaching out over the Thames. The room upstairs is where Marc Brunel held meetings trying to raise cash to continue the Tunnel.

To get home, there are two options. One is to return to Rotherhithe Station and take the overground line south to Surrey Quays for the Jubilee line, or north to Whitechapel for the Elizabeth, District or Metropolitan line. Alternatively, you could walk along the river back to Tower Bridge. It's less than 2 miles and the route is covered, in part, by the last walk in this book.

FURTHER EXCURSIONS

If you wanted to visit the family grave of this remarkable family, you'll find them at Kensal Green, one of the great Victorian Cemeteries.

For Isambard's train engineering, you could visit Paddington Station, the terminus of the Great Western Railway where the ironwork is still original. Better still, why not jump on a train down to Bristol where you can see the SS Great Britain, the only one of Isambard's great ships still in existence.

6. CHARLES DICKENS AND VICTORIAN LONDON

If there is one person who has shaped and coloured our imagination of Victorian London, it's probably Charles Dickens. In his novels and articles, he wrote about a London that was teeming with life, full of heroes and villains, benefactors and criminals, maidens and prostitutes. Unforgettable characters like Fagin, Scrooge, Uriah Heep, Tiny Tim and Little Nell were drawn from the streets of London and the city itself became a character in his novels with its pea-souper fogs, its mud and its stench.

Like so many other great Londoners, Dickens wasn't born in the city. Instead, he was born in Portsmouth, the son of a clerk in the Royal Navy. The family followed the father around, finally settling in London in 1822 when Charles was 10. Disaster soon struck when his father was taken to the Marshalsea Debtors Prison for spending way beyond his means. Charles was taken from school and sent to work 10 hour days at Warren's Blacking Factory. The shame and perceived injustice of his position had a lasting effect on Dickens, sparking his interest and concern in the plight of children in 19th century London.

He later returned to school for a couple of years but left education for good at 15 and took a job as a clerk in a law firm in Gray's Inn. He started reporting on legal cases and this led him to a post as a parliamentary reporter. He was a prodigious writer, not only contributing political sketches but reporting on the people he met on the streets of London. These were published under the title of 'Sketches by Boz' and his name began to be known in publishing circles. However, his career really took off when he began to write 'The Pickwick Papers'.

The book has been called 'the most important single novel of the Victorian era' because it transformed literature from a pursuit of the leisured classes into entertainment for all. Eventually, almost everybody enjoyed Dickens, from Queen Victoria to illiterate working men who would pay a halfpenny to have the latest chapter read to them. His novels came out in monthly instalments, printed in magazines with cliff-hangers to keep his readers engrossed. In his twenties, he wrote a string of literary blockbusters: Oliver Twist, Nicholas Nickleby, The Old Curiosity Shop and Barnaby Rudge. By the time he was 28, he was one of the most famous men in Britain, lauded wherever he went.

Dickens had married Catherine Hogarth and over the next 15 years she bore 11 children. As his family and wealth increased, Dickens moved into increasingly grand homes culminating in Tavistock House on Tavistock Square.

Book after book came out in rapid succession and Dickens became an international superstar. He travelled frequently, especially to France and to North America. It's hard to overestimate what a sensation Dickens was. At a reception for him in New York, when he was not yet aged 30, 3,000 people paid to see him at an event hosted by the Mayor, and Dickens went on to meet the US president. Similarly in France he became very well known and met luminaries such as Victor Hugo and Alexandre Dumas.

At home he worked frenetically. Apart from publishing his novels, 18 in as many years, he also owned and edited magazines, writing hundreds of articles and letters each year, put on and acted in plays and went on reading tours. He was a great social campaigner, protesting against the evils that he saw on the streets of London. He wrote against public executions, the Crimean War, the state of Smithfield market and dozens of other issues. His greatest novels are protests about the way society treated the poor and especially the plight of children. So Oliver Twist highlighted the brutal and inhumane way workhouses operated and Nicholas Nickleby exposed and mocked the state of education. He worked closely with the great social reformer of Victorian England, Angela Burdett Coutts, on many of her projects, helping set up Ragged Schools and creating 'a home' where women involved in prostitution could break from their former life, learn new skills and, if they wanted, be helped to emigrate to the colonies.

Dickens still had energy to spare. Often at night he would pound the streets of London, sometimes walking 20 miles in a night. He went everywhere, especially areas outside of respectable London. He often ended up in the East End or down by the river and he used the names, places and faces for his novels. There are plenty of gazetteers of Dickens' London and they contain hundreds of place names which feature in his novels. The Pickwick Papers, for instance, mentions over 100 sites in

London where the action is set. He stole the names of streets, the people he had once known and great London institutions to reflect the city back on its inhabitants. They loved it and they loved him.

By the 1850's, however, his domestic life was increasingly unhappy. He had met and become infatuated with a young actress, Ellen Ternan, who at 17 was nearly 30 years younger than him. Dickens even went to the lengths of partitioning the marital bedroom down the middle, a pretty clear sign that the marriage was over. He eventually separated from his wife but would not divorce her as he thought the inevitable scandal would alienate his fans. He kept his relationship with Ellen secret but he cut Catherine off, gave her an allowance and never saw her again.

Increasingly, Dickens lived in Kent where he bought a mansion at Gad's Hill, but he came frequently to London to edit his magazines and oversee his many business and charitable interests. His appetite for work remained prodigious. Although he was a wealthy man, he continued to undertake punishing lecture tours where he would read extracts from his works. He continued with these despite rapidly declining health. In June 1870, aged only 58, he died. He was buried, not as he wished, in a quiet Kent church, but, after a Times editorial, amongst the great and good in Poets Corner in Westminster Abbey. Tens of thousands filed past the grave. The news of his death reverberated around the world; Longfellow wrote from America that *'It is no exaggeration to say that this whole country is stricken with grief'*.

So Dickens died; the greatest author and one of the greatest entertainers the capital has ever had. His evocation of Victorian London still permeates our modern view of this extraordinary city.

FURTHER READING

There are hundreds of books on Dickens and a fair few that outline Dickens-themed walks in London. A good introduction is *Dickens: Public Life and Private Passion,* by Peter Ackroyd, or there is the magisterial *Charles Dickens: A Life,* by Claire Tomalin.

THE WALK

On this walk we follow in Dickens' footsteps from his traumatic early life and his brief career in the law, to the house where he became first a literary superstar and then one of the great men of Victorian London. It's best to do this during a weekday. At weekends the two great Inns of Court that we visit, and which are very atmospheric, are both closed.

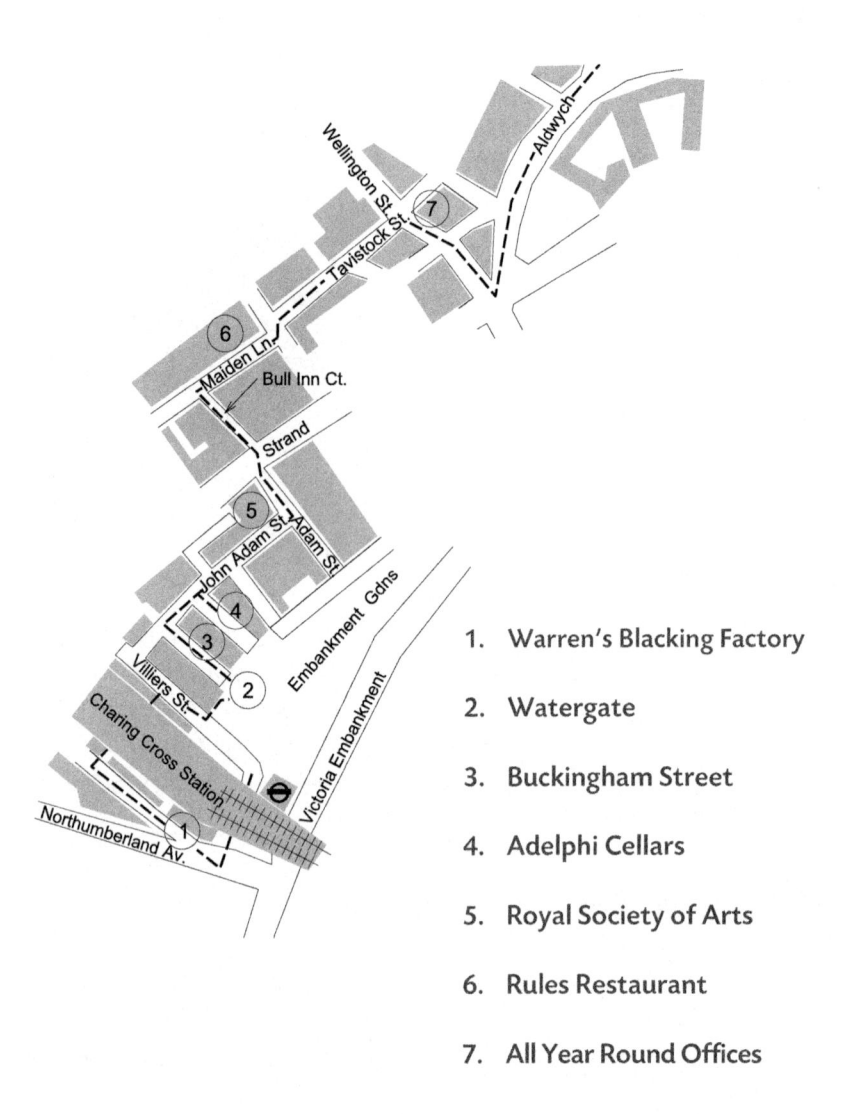

1. Warren's Blacking Factory
2. Watergate
3. Buckingham Street
4. Adelphi Cellars
5. Royal Society of Arts
6. Rules Restaurant
7. All Year Round Offices

THE ROUTE

We start at Embankment Station in Villiers Street and walk under the railway tracks to the corner of Craven Street and Northumberland Avenue.

Stop 1

The nondescript service entrance in front of you is the approximate site of Warren's Blacking Factory where Dickens was sent to work at the age of 12 after his father was imprisoned for debt. Then the factory overlooked the river and was overrun with rats. The experience scarred Dickens for life and it permeates many of his stories. One of his workmates was called Bob Fagin, later immortalised in Oliver Twist.

Walk up Craven Street, which has a proud literary history, with plaques to Heinrich Heine and Benjamin Franklin.

Halfway up the street we take a right through Craven Passage. We pass the Ship and Shovell, the only pub in London housed in two separate buildings. They're on opposite sides of the street but connected by an underground passage. The houses date back to 1731, so Dickens would have certainly passed them even if he did not drink in them.

We turn right at Villiers Street, noticing a plaque to Rudyard Kipling and then turn left at Gordon's Wine Bar, one of the most atmospheric drinking haunts in London. In the gardens on your right you come to York Watergate.

Stop 2

This is an extraordinary remnant of a time long passed. It was the river entrance to the great house of the Duke of Buckingham. It dates back to 1626 but is now marooned 150 yards from the river after the building of the Embankment. A number of the streets behind the watergate are named after the Villiers family, the Dukes of Buckingham.

We walk back up the steps and enter Buckingham Street.

Stop 3

Dickens lived at no. 17 Buckingham Street when he was working as parliamentary reporter in Westminster; his autobiographical creation, David Copperfield, was also deemed to have lived there. There's a plaque as well to Samuel Pepys.

Walk up the street and turn right into John Adam Street, named after the great 18th century architect. Much of this area was designed by the Adam brothers; John, James, William and Robert in the 1770s.

Take a right down York Buildings and on your left is the entrance to the cellars of the Adelphi complex built by the Adam brothers (Adelphi means brothers in Greek). This involved a block of 24 grand houses fronting onto the Thames with warehousing underneath. It was never a great success and in the 1930's much of the terrace was demolished to make way for the current Art Deco Adelphi House.

Stop 4

Today, the entry to the cellars is a road leading down to the river but it's very rarely used except by taxi drivers taking a short cut to the Embankment. Dickens described exploring it as a young man in David Copperfield. If you really want to walk in his footsteps, you too can go exploring, but it's a bit smelly and not very edifying. So instead we retrace our footsteps and continue walking along John Adam Street.

Stop 5

Stop outside the Royal Society of Arts building. This is one of the Adam brothers' houses, as is Adam House facing down the street. Dickens was a Fellow of the RSA and so would have visited the house. Other Fellows were Karl Marx, Benjamin Franklin, William Hogarth and in more modern times, Nelson Mandela, Judi Dench and David Attenborough. The house has been expanded and includes the Adelphi Tavern mentioned in the Pickwick Papers.

Continue walking along John Adam Street and then turn left along Adam Street and cross the Strand. In front of you there is the entrance to a tiny and very atmospheric alley, Bull Inn Court with a fine pub. Walk through it and then turn right into Maiden Lane. J M W Turner was born here in 1775.

Stop 6

Walk down the Lane until you reach, on your left, Rules Restaurant. Rules claims to be London's oldest restaurant, dating back to 1798. Dickens dined here many times and there is a private dining room named after him. Another frequent visitor was the future Edward VII with his mistress, Lily Langtry, and they are similarly honoured.

Cross Southampton Street then walk down Tavistock Street which is almost opposite. Stop on the corner of Wellington Street.

Stop 7

In front of you are the London offices of the magazine 'All Year Round', that Dickens owned and ran. But it also housed his London apartment after the end of his marriage to Catherine. By now, Dickens was living in Kent and in a relationship with Ellen Ternan and this was his base when he came back to the city. Turn right into Aldwych and walk left to cross Kingsway and then turn left to walk towards Holborn.

Turn right into Portugal Street.

84   Walking with Londoners

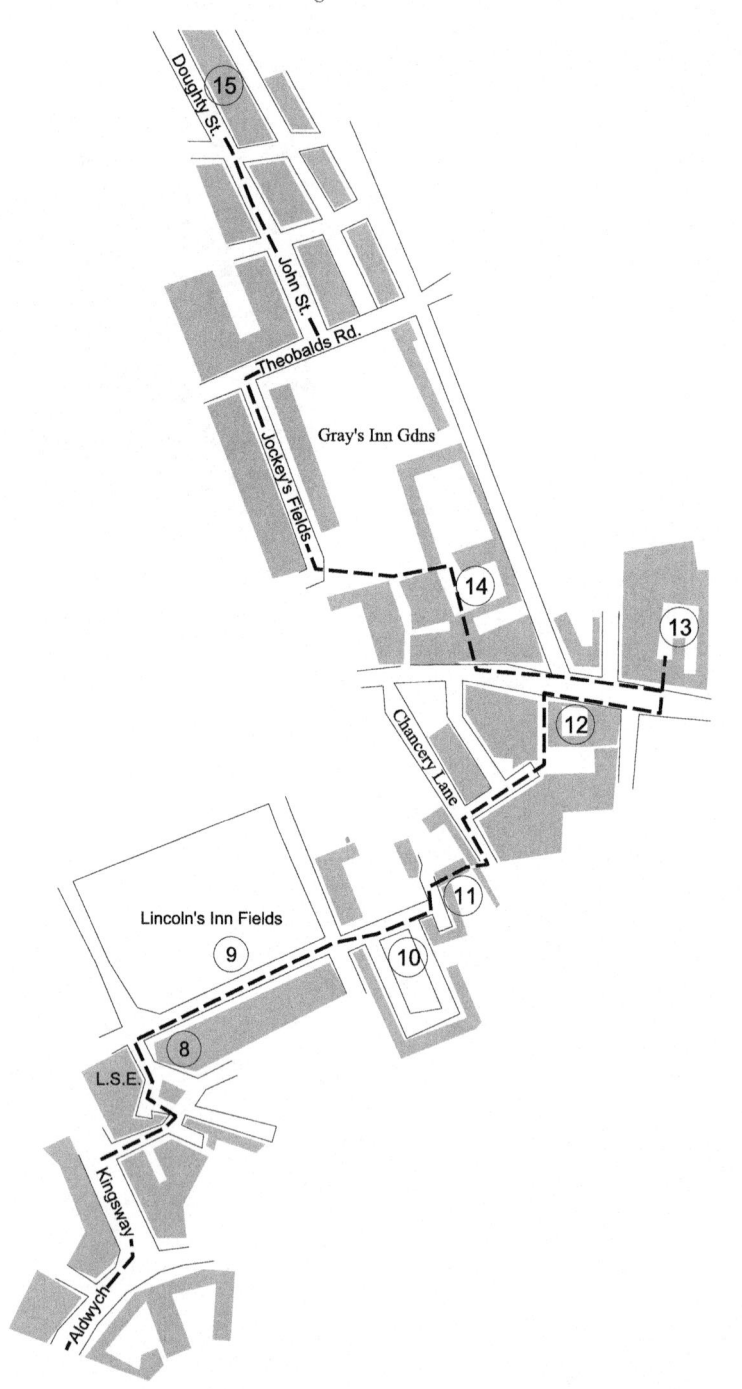

8. Old Curiosity Shop   12. Staple Inn

9. Lincoln's Inn Fields   13. Furnival's Inn

10. Lincoln's Inn   14. Gray's Inn

11. Old Hall   15. Dickens' Museum

Stop 8
As you walk into the campus of the London School of Economics, diagonally to your left you will see a very old building labelled 'The Old Curiosity Shop' which dates back to 1567. Dickens wrote the melodrama at the peak of his fame and it concerns the life and death of Little Nell who supposedly worked in the shop. The book was a sensation. Published in serial form it entranced most, though not all, of its readers. (Oscar Wilde famously wrote: *'One would have to have a heart of stone to read the death of Little Nell without dissolving into tears ... of laughter'.*) Unfortunately, the shop we're looking at is unlikely to have been the model for Dickens as he wrote that it had been pulled down many years previously.

Just to the left of the shop you'll see Lincoln Inn Fields to which we now head.

Stop 9
Lincolns Inn Fields is full of delights. On the north side of the square is the wonderful Sir John Soane Museum and on the south, the somewhat gruesome Hunterian Museum of the Royal College of Surgeons. We are interested, however, in the west side where at no. 57 was the house of John Foster. He played an important role in bringing the young Dickens to the notice of

London society, became his best friend and went on to publish the first, and most important, biography of the author.

Walk to the east side of Lincoln's Inn Fields and in the south east corner you see the entrance to the Lincoln's Inn itself. NB Lincoln's Inn is not open at the weekends. If it's closed you'll need to rejoin the walk at stop 12.

Stop 10

Lincoln's Inn is one of the four great Inns of Court, the bodies to which all barristers belong. The other three are Gray's Inn and the Middle and Inner Temple. Lincoln's Inn was definitely in existence in 1422 and probably dates back another 100 years before then. All the Inns of Court were well known to Dickens when he worked as a legal assistant, as one of his tasks was to take documents between the various offices. Indeed, he set the opening scene of Bleak House in Lincoln's Inn.

There is much to see in the complex, although not all is open to the public, even during the week. The building on the left as you walk in is the Great Hall in a Tudor style, though in fact it is Victorian. On the right is New Square, although it is really quite old, dating back to the 1680s.

As you walk through you come to the heart of the original Lincoln's Inn.

Stop 11

In front of you is the Old Hall, dating back to at least 1489. It is not normally open to the public.

Next to it on the left is a wonderful chapel dating to the 1620's and designed by Inigo Jones. It stands above an undercroft where old members of the Inn are buried. Its most famous preacher was John Donne, the great metaphysical poet. It was, and is, a tradition at Lincoln's Inn that upon the death of a member a bell would toll and lawyers would send their clerks to find out who had died. This inspired the famous poem by Donne that starts *'No man is an island'* and finishes with *'never send to know for whom the bell tolls, it tolls for thee'*.

Walk through the undercroft right towards the Main Gate. Legend has it that Ben Jonson, contemporary and rival of Shakespeare, worked on the walls as a bricklayer before finding fame as a playwright. This is the oldest part of the inn, and parts of the square date back to the 15th century. Exit in to Chancery Lane (if the door is locked you'll have to retrace your steps and then walk through Stone Buildings) and turn left. Turn right into Southampton Buildings and walk through Staple Inn. Since the Covid Pandemic, this route has sometimes been prohibited to the passer-by. If there is a sign prohibiting entry, simply carry on walking through the ornamental gateway and you'll come out onto High Holborn by Chancery Lane station. A 'Staple', by the way, was the measurement of a sack of wool, the heart of the medieval economy.

Stop 12
The Tudor looking buildings you're standing next to are, in fact, Tudor. Most people assume that they're mock Victorian but they do date back to the middle of the 16th century. Staple Inn was an Inn of Chancery, essentially a preparatory school before admission to an Inn of Court. Dickens wrote about the little square behind the great gate as a place where the sounds of the city disappear. That's still the case today.

Walk east down High Holborn and within a hundred yards or so, you come to Barnards Inn, another inn of chancery. This houses Gresham College, founded in 1597, who put on an annual series of expert lectures. As you walk through you will see its hall which dates from the 15th century but rests on Roman foundations. In Great Expectations, Pip stayed here when he arrived in London.

Retrace your steps and cross High Holborn to the magnificent red brick building opposite and go inside.

Stop 13
The red bricks formed one of the most famous buildings in London; the old Prudential Insurance. It was built in the late 1870's, but before then it was the site of Furnival's Inn, another Inn of Chancery. It was where Charles and Catherine Dickens first set up as a married couple. Dickens was to describe that period as being the

happiest time of his life. It was also where his fame began as he worked on the Pickwick Papers; the book which made his name.

As you walk through the first arch you'll see a plaque to Dickens high up on the wall to your right. Go into the great courtyard and on the back wall in the left hand corner is a bust of Dickens in a small alcove.

Come out of the building and walk west along High Holborn, watching out for an entrance into Gray's Inn on your right, and walk through.

Stop 14

You enter into South Square. Gray's Inn goes back to at least the 14th century. Opposite you is the Great Hall where Shakespeare premiered The Comedy of Errors and to its right is the chapel. The complex of buildings dates back to Tudor times, although much was rebuilt in the late 17th century, and it was badly damaged in the Blitz.

It was also the site of Dickens' first job. He was employed as a legal clerk at the age of 15 at no.1 South Square, near where you entered. Being young and bored, he apparently used to amuse himself by entertaining his fellow clerks with impressions and by dropping cherry stones on passers-by beneath his window. But it was also here that he learnt shorthand, became a parliamentary reporter and started writing sketches on London life.

Walk through into North Square and then through an alley on your left. Notice the watchman's stool as you enter. You pass by The Walks which were laid out at the end of the 16th century. Pepys used to stroll here to admire the ladies. You can walk through them at lunch time and then exit in the top left hand corner. Otherwise, carry on past the entrance to the walks and after a few buildings, turn into the street on your right and walk to the end.

You leave Gray's Inn at the corner of Jockey's Fields and Theobald's Road, turn right along Theobalds Road and turn left up John Street and onto Doughty Street.

Stop 15
On your right, you'll find the wonderful Charles Dickens Museum at no. 48 Doughty Street. Here he finished Pickwick Papers and started writing the blockbuster that became Oliver Twist. Royalties poured in and he was able to take his growing family to much grander houses near Regents Park and then on Tavistock Square. The museum is laid out as if Dickens had just popped out. The table is set for dinner, his shadow is on the stairs and his study is laid out ready for work. For details see **www.dickensmuseum.com**. It's well worth visiting and a fitting end to our walk.

AND FINALLY

Just at the back of the museum is a fine pub – the Old Blue Lion. It's in Brownlow Mews, and Brownlow is the name of the man who rescues our hero at the end of Oliver Twist. Dickens must have drank here while writing Oliver Twist.

Nearest stations are Kings Cross or Chancery Lane at either end of Gray's Inn Road.

FURTHER EXCURSIONS

It's almost impossible to go anywhere in central London without stumbling over a pub or building used by Dickens as a setting for one of his novels. There are many books and websites specialising in Dickensian London.

Try **www.charlesdickenspage.com**

A good day trip would be to visit another Dickens Museum, this time on the Kent coast at Broadstairs or, a bit nearer, the Guildhall Museum in Rochester which has a permanent exhibition on Dickens.

7. KARL MARX AND THE STREETS OF SOHO AND BLOOMSBURY

Over the centuries, London has absorbed waves of refugees fleeing persecution, repression or poverty from all over the world. They have not always been welcomed, but all have contributed to the city's rich heritage.

Perhaps the most famous, certainly the most influential refugee of all, was Karl Marx, the great theorist of capitalism and philosopher of communism. He was born in Trier in Germany in 1818 and, as a young man, went to the University of Bonn where he came into contact with the radical university groups that flourished in Germany of the 1840s. By the time he was 24, he was a full time political activist, and exiled from Germany. He was also married to Jenny von Westphalen, daughter of a German Baron and descended from the Dukes of Argyll. It was the start of a long and devoted marriage but one also marred by grinding poverty and infidelity. Marx finally arrived in London as a political exile at the age of 31. He was to remain there until his death in 1883 at the age of 64. He thus spent more than half his life in London and it was there that he wrote the works for which he was most famous, especially The Communist Manifesto and Das Kapital. It was said of Marx that he learnt his philosophy in Germany, his politics in France and his economics in England. There is a strand of truth in this, but he brought all these elements together in London, and it was in London where his political activism laid down the building blocks of the great Marxist parties which flourished across Europe 30 years after his death.

The turning point in Marx's life came in 1848 as revolutions broke out across Europe. Marx and his friend and collaborator, Friedrich Engels, threw themselves into the struggle, moving between the capitals of Europe. They visited London where they were commissioned to write a statement of aims for the German Workers Educational Association, a group of German emigres based in a pub in Great Windmill Street, Soho. What emerged was one of the most famous books in history: the Communist Manifesto. Published in German by a printer near Liverpool

Street, it was largely ignored and had little or no impact on the revolutions of 1848. But within a few decades it became one of the most influential books ever written.

The revolutions were crushed across Europe and Marx was expelled successively from Germany, Belgium and France. Finally, he, along with Jenny and their three children, arrived in London in the late summer of 1849. Their first house was in fashionable Chelsea at 4 Anderson Terrace, but it was not to last. It was far too expensive for a professional revolutionary. Debts mounted: Karl wasn't earning and Jenny had just given birth to their fourth child. The Marxes were unceremoniously evicted under the eyes of a delighted crowd. All their possessions were sold and the family fled to the Hotel du Commerce in Leicester Street. But hotel living was even more expensive and in Jenny's words *'one morning our host refused to serve us our breakfast and we were forced to look for other lodgings'.*

The Marxes found their first real home just round the corner from the hotel at 64 Dean Street in Soho. They spent a miserable summer there, but a few months later they moved just up the street to number 28. There, the expanding family lived in two rooms for the next six years. It was a very tight fit indeed. One of the rooms served as Karl's study and besides Jenny, and by now five children, there was also Helene Delmuth, their housekeeper. It must have been very crowded and one wonders how on earth Karl and Helene found the space and opportunity to conceive a child together. The scandal was hushed up and the little boy was sent to foster parents with Engels implicitly accepting paternity.

The Marx family, during the 1850's, was desperately poor, only kept going by the generosity of Engels who was working in the family firm in Manchester. Despite his subventions, Marx was a frequent visitor to pawn brokers, having to pawn his clothes to raise money for food. At other times, he fled from Soho to avoid creditors.

Soho was an appropriate place for the Marxes. It was home to many European immigrants attracted by the area's cheap housing. Many of them worked in the local restaurants, and there was a thriving cultural scene. But most of all, it was a place for the poor. The inadequate water supply and the appalling sewage system meant that cholera and other diseases were rampant. Three of the Marx children, Henry, Franziska and Edgar, died in infancy in Dean Street. Marx earned a precarious living writing articles for the New York Daily Tribune on current affairs. Most of his time, however, was spent researching economics in the British Museum. This culminated with the publication of volume one of his master work, Das Kapital, first published in 1867.

These terrible years of poverty lasted until 1856 when Jenny inherited money from relatives which allowed the family to escape to the developing north London suburbs of Kentish Town and Chalk Farm. Their first house was in Grafton Terrace and still survives. There's no plaque on the wall but, appropriately, the front door is painted brightest red. Later, the family moved successively to no. 1 and then 41 Maitland Park Road where both Jenny, and then Karl, died. Both houses have since disappeared with only a plaque reminding us that the great revolutionary lived there in petty bourgeois respectability.

While Marx had left the hurly burly of the streets of Soho, he began to immerse himself once again in political activity in the 1860's. The British Labour Movement, after a decade or more of quiet, began to stir. The trade unions began to grow once more amongst skilled workers, especially engineers and construction workers. Events from outside the country, especially the American Civil War and the visit of the great Italian freedom fighter, Garibaldi, led to a general upsurge and interest in political change. In 1864, a conference was held in St. Martin's Hall in Covent Garden with a number of delegations from the continent. Marx was invited to write the Inaugural Address of what became The International Working Men's Association. The IWMA was a lively affair, meeting regularly in Greek Street in Soho and organising social events such as a soiree with tea, singing by choirs of German and Italian working men and dancing '3 polkas, 3 quadrilles and 12 other dances'.

The uprising of the Paris Commune of 1870 gave a fresh impetus to Marx's activity. He and his three daughters, Jenny, Laura and Eleanor, threw themselves into the work of supporting the flood of refugees who came to London after the defeat of the Commune. The fall of the Commune had a very direct impact on the Marx family: Jenny, Marx's eldest daughter, married Charles Longuet, a refugee from the fighting; Laura, Marx's second daughter, married Paul Lafargue who had been banned from all French universities even before the uprising. Finally, Eleanor, the youngest daughter, engaged in a passionate love affair with Prosper-Olivier Lissagaray, a fighter for the Communards. Marx was outraged that his 17-year-old daughter had fallen in love with a man twice her age. The relationship lasted seven years but when Karl finally gave his approval to the match, Eleanor called the relationship off.

The First International, as it came to be called, was never a mass organisation and came to an end within 10 years of its formation but it did form a model for the 'Second International', founded in 1889, in which Eleanor was heavily involved. This brought together the mass workers' parties in France, Germany, Italy, Russia and many other countries, which was the main channel through which Marxist theories became part of the political landscape.

For the last 10 years of his life, Marx lived increasingly quietly in north London. As his financial troubles eased, thanks to increasing subsidies from Engels, his health began to decline. A heavy drinker and smoker, he was plagued by boils. In the early 1880's, Marx was struck by two tragedies: first his wife, Jenny, died of liver cancer and then his firstborn, also called Jenny, died of cancer aged only 38. Karl never recovered from these losses and within two months of his daughter's death, he, too, died. Husband and wife were buried in a simple family grave in Highgate Cemetery. Karl's funeral was a small affair attended by only around 20 people. 70 years later, he was reinterred under an enormous bust, commissioned and paid for by the Communist Party of the USSR, with the ceremony led by Nikita Krushchev. The plinth bears the famous exhortation *'Workers of all lands, unite'*.

The Marxist tradition in Britain was carried on by a small band of followers, principally Friedrich Engels and Eleanor. Engels lived on for another 12 years at 122 Regents Park Road, editing 2 more volumes of Das Kapital, writing works on the family and state and acting both as Marx's executor and as a father figure to Marx's surviving daughters.

Eleanor, the youngest daughter, became very well known in Britain's socialist movement. She worked and argued with some of the leading lights of the early socialist movement such as William Morris, Annie Besant, Keir Hardie and George Bernard Shaw. She was also actively involved in the developing mass union movement of the late 1880's, active in the strikes of the gas workers and dockers, amongst many others. She helped organise and spoke at the first mass May Day demonstrations, including to an audience of 250,000 demanding the 8 hour day in 1890. She was also active internationally, helping to set up the Second International, which propagated her father's ideas across Europe, the Americas, and crucially, Russia.

Eleanor was far more than just a political activist. She was a talented linguist, speaking English, German and French fluently. She learnt Yiddish in order to work with the Jewish garment workers of the East End and Norwegian so that she could translate the plays of Henrik Ibsen. She was also the first translator of Flaubert's Madame Bovary.

But for all her activism and political confidence, her personal life was a disaster. She fell in love with Edward Aveling, a leading figure in the early socialist movement in London. He was married to a wealthy heiress but lived apart. For almost 15 years Eleanor lived with him, defying bourgeois convention. Aveling was despised by many in the socialist movement. He had been accused of stealing money from the movement and was widely distrusted. Sylvia Pankhurst, who met him while a young adolescent, thought of him as 'reptilian'. Despite the warnings and his frequent infidelity, Eleanor stayed with him. After Aveling's first wife died, leaving him free to marry again, Eleanor was horrified to learn that he had secretly married an actress with whom he had been having an affair. A few months after learning the news, Eleanor committed suicide by swallowing prussic acid. She was 43. She was cremated and her ashes finally reunited with her mother and father in 1956 in the grave in Highgate Cemetery.

FURTHER READING

A couple of good books which explore the personalities as well as the politics are:

Karl Marx, by Francis Wheen

Eleanor Marx: A Life, by Rachel Holmes

THE WALK

On this walk we explore the backstreets of Soho where the Marx family endured terrible poverty in the 1850's. We walk through Fitzrovia, a stronghold of communist and anarchist thought and where both Karl and Eleanor met, plotted and drank the night away. Finally, we end in Bloomsbury and the British Museum where Marx spent years writing Das Kapital.

1. Hotel du Commerce
2. Communards' Club
3. Old Red Lion
4. John Snow Pump
5. 64 Dean Street
6. 26 Dean Street
7. IWMA HQ
8. Soho Square

7. Karl Marx and the Streets of Soho and Bloomsbury

THE ROUTE

We start in Leicester Square and walk through Leicester Place. This has been the centre of London's entertainment district for at least 200 years. At the site of no. 5 was Burford's Panorama, which exhibited historic scenes for the entertainment of Londoners. It was in existence when Marx was living nearby, offering a diorama of the Crimean War. Today it is a French church and inside there are some wonderful murals by Jean Cocteau.

Turn left down Lisle Street and at the next corner on the left, Leicester Street, is our first stop.

Stop 1

The building on our left once housed the Hotel du Commerce and on its wall there is a plaque commemorating the stay of Johann Strauss. But it was also the lodging house where Karl and Jenny sheltered for a few days until they were once again evicted into the streets of Soho.

Keep walking down Lisle Street and right into Wardour Street. Look up and you'll see ghostly reminders of the old Soho, of the people who once lived and worked here. For instance, you'll see signs saying 'Pinolo' or 'Bullion Office' dating back to the 19th century. Walk right along Wardour Street and then go through the little passageway of Rupert Court on your left. As you walk through, glance up and you'll see a sign reading Ancient Lights above a building straddling the alley. This meant that there was a right to light so builders weren't allowed to block it out. We'll see another one later in the walk.

Turn right into Rupert Street.

Stop 2

Currently a restaurant, Hovarda, 36-40 Rupert Street was once a Communards Club. After the destruction of the Paris Commune by government troops, some thousands of political refugees arrived in London. Marx and Eleanor threw themselves into the aid effort, housing, feeding and supporting the exiles.

Cross Shaftesbury Avenue, continue walking up Rupert Street, turn left into Archer Street.

At the end of the street on the corner of Great Windmill Street, you have, politically at least, one of the most important pubs in London.

Stop 3

Today it is called Be At One, but in Marx's time it was The Old Red Lion. In 1847 it was the headquarters of the German Workers Educational Association, a branch of Marx's Communist League. They commissioned Marx and Engels to write a profession of faith. It took six months for the pair to get round to writing the pamphlet but once Marx got stuck in, he produced the Communist Manifesto in a few days. One of the most widely read and influential works ever written, it had almost no impact on the revolutions breaking out all over Europe in 1848.

The Old Red Lion remained at the centre of Marx's political and social life for the next few years. He often lectured here on political economy or Greek and Latin but there were also activities like singing, dancing and, of course, drinking.

Walk right up Great Windmill Street, cross Brewer Street and continue up Lexington Street and reach Broadwick Street.

Stop 4

You're standing by the John Snow Pub, named after a contemporary of Marx and one of the great heroes of Victorian medical science. Soho in the 1840's and 1850's was ravaged by outbreaks of cholera when hundreds, sometimes thousands, died. The thinking at the time was that cholera was spread by air, the so-called miasma theory. If something smelled bad you could catch it. John Snow, by patient data analysis of cholera outbreaks, showed that it was being spread by water pollution. He had the handle of the pump removed, forcing the local people to go elsewhere to access cleaner water. A replica of the pump is still there outside the pub, sans handle. Snow died young but for his work in Soho he has been called the father of modern epidemiology.

Walk right down Broadwick Street and then right along Berwick Street. Berwick Street still has its street market which dates back 250 years. Once it provided the staples for this working class neighbourhood; today it provides food from around the world to the media workers and tourists who frequent lunchtime Soho.

Go through the alleyway at the bottom, which once hosted Raymond Revue Bar, and turn left along Brewer Street, cross Wardour Street and then along Old Compton Street, just to your right.

Turn left into Dean Street.

Stop 5
Stop outside No. 64. On this site was the Marx's first Soho apartment after they had been ejected from the hotel in Leicester Street. The building no longer exists but its next door neighbour is a beautiful example of an old Soho house and probably very similar. The Marxes rented two rooms; Jenny was pregnant again and they were desperately poor. At the end of 1850, they moved 100 yards up the street to no. 26 Dean Street. We walk up Dean Street.

Stop 6
It's now a fancy restaurant, Quo Vadis, but the Marxes lived here in abject poverty. The family rented two rooms on the top floor. The whole family, including Helene Demuth, slept in one small room while the other was ostensibly Karl's study but also the children's play room, the dining room and where Marx met his many visitors. You'll see a plaque on the wall which unfortunately gets the dates wrong. They moved here in 1850, not 1851. In the window of Quo Vadis you'll see a poster mentioning the family's stay here.

Retrace your steps and turn left down Bateman Street then right down Frith Street passing Ronnie Scott's and Bar Italia. Go left down Old Compton Street and first left down Greek Street. Stop outside no. 18.

Stop 7

This was the headquarters of the International Working Men's Association, formed by Marx and English trade unionists, and French and Italian socialists, in 1864. Marx ended up as the German secretary for the IWMA and wrote its rules and principles. The First International had a limited impact but it lay the foundations for the Second International where the ideas of Marxism were spread across Europe by the great continental social democratic parties of Germany, France, Italy and, especially, Russia. (Remember the Bolsheviks official title was the Russian Social Democratic Party.) There is a plaque on the wall but it is to the late, great Peter Cook who was, in his way, almost as subversive as the socialists who once gathered here.

Continue walking up Greek Street until you arrive in Soho Square. As you enter Soho Square you are next to the wonderful House of St. Barnabas which dates back to the 1740's. It was once the property of the Beckford family who were plantation and slave owners. It then became the offices of Joseph Bazalgette when he was designing London's sewers (see next chapter). Since the 1860's, the house has been used as a charity for the homeless. Today it is a private members' club where the profits help people make a fresh start. At its front there is a unique system of receiving donations which still works.

Move into Soho Square.

Stop 8

We're now in the very centre of Soho, and this square was laid out in the 1670's when Soho was on the edge of London and the rich and wealthy were beginning to migrate west out of the city devastated by the Great Fire. For a while it became one of the most fashionable addresses in London, but by Marx's time it had gone down in the world.

A statue of Charles II stands in the middle of the square, looking somewhat weather-beaten. Behind it is a strange little mock-Tudor hut which hides an electricity sub-station. Only a few of the houses, notably nos. 10 and 15, date back to the 17th century and they have been significantly modernised. The most interesting buildings are the French Protestant Church in the north west corner which serviced the spiritual needs of the emigres who congregated in Soho, and the Hospital for Women which opened a year after the Marx's arrival. There is also a blue plaque commemorating Mary Seacole, the Jamaican nurse who set up a hospital in the Crimea and has been recently voted the greatest black Briton.

Leave the square heading north along Soho Street, cross Oxford Street and walk into Rathbone Place.

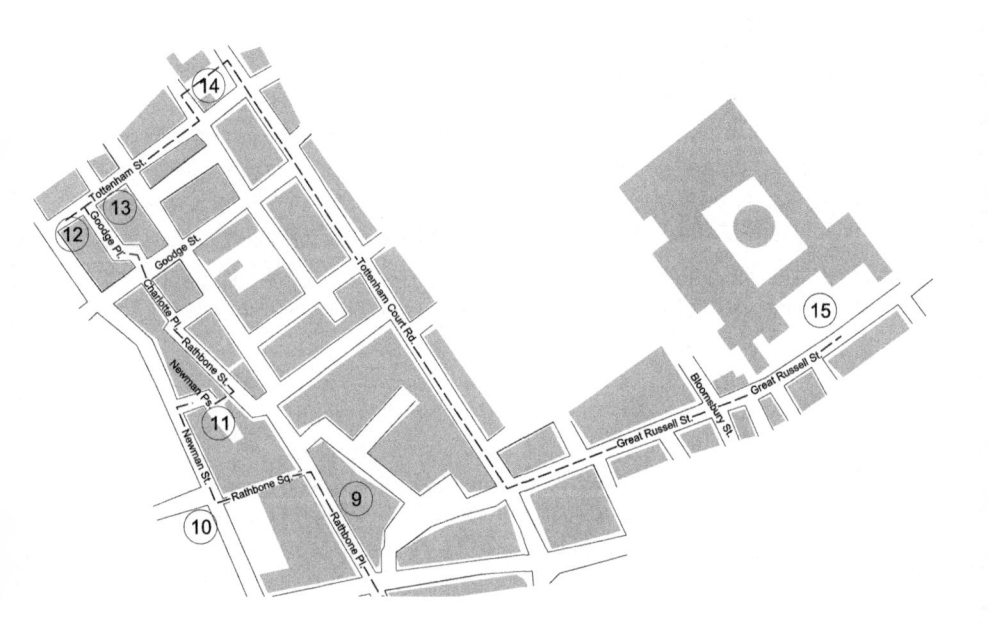

9. Fitzrovia

10. Blue Posts

11. Newman Passage

12. Communist Working Men's Club

13. Equiano Plaque

14. Whitfield Gardens

15. British Museum

Stop 9

We're now in Fitzrovia, which for around a century after 1850, was home to London's bohemia. The list of those who lived here is a roll call of famous names: Virginia Woolf, George Bernard Shaw, Walter Sickert, Augustus John, George Orwell, Dylan Thomas and Graham Greene for starters. It was also the place where European migrants tended to concentrate, as many worked in the restaurants of the West End. It was a natural hangout for radicals of all descriptions who patronised the cafés, and especially the many pubs, of the area.

This street hosted the fencing salon of Emanuel Barthelemy which Marx used to frequent in the 1850's. Apparently what Marx *'lacked in science, he tried to make up in aggression'*. In the 1870's, there were dozens of political clubs operating in the little alleys and mews of Fitzrovia. At the top of Rathbone Place, for instance, in Stephen Mews, there was Club Autonomie, catering mainly for French Anarchists, while almost next door in Percy Mews, the IWMA had a drinking den.

After a few hundred yards there's an entrance on the left to the modern development of Rathbone Square. Walk through it into Newman Street and opposite there is another famous political pub: The Blue Posts.

Stop 10

This pub hosted the final London meeting of the General Council of the First International in 1871. By now, the IWMA was irrevocably split between an anarchist wing led by Mikhail Bakunin and the Marxian wing. Within a year the organisation was no more.

Walk up Newman Street and on your right, after 100 yards, turn down Newman Passage. This little alley takes you back 150 years or more, a real lost world, redolent of a very different time.

Stop 11

The passage opens into a small square with another 'Ancient Lights' sign. In 1871, a Communard kitchen was based here, feeding the Parisian refugees, and it was near here that Eleanor Marx met Prosper Lissagaray; the first great love of her life.

Walk through the passage past the Newman Arms (which was the model for

The Proles pub in Orwell's 1984) and turn left into Rathbone Street. Glance back at the top windows of the pub where a Georgian lady beckons you in, reminding us that the pub used to be a brothel, 250 years ago. Walk along Rathbone Street through Charlotte Place, cross Goodge Street, into Goodge Place and then turn left into Tottenham Street.

Stop 12
At no. 49 is the site of one of Marx's favourite drinking spots. It had a number of names but Marx knew it as the Communist Working Men's Club. Many of the great names of the socialist movement drank here, including Karl and Eleanor, Engels, George Bernard Shaw, Keir Hardie and William Morris.

Retrace your steps and on your right is a blue plaque at no.37 Tottenham Street commemorating Olaudah Equiano, the great publicist and fighter for the abolition of the slave trade.

Stop 13
A freed slave, Equiano wrote his autobiography which laid bare the savagery of the slave trade and conditions in the plantations. It was a best seller and contributed greatly to the rise of the abolitionist movement.

Walk to the corner of Whitfield Street, turn left and there is an open space on the right.

Stop 14
This is the site of a cemetery attached to Whitfield's Tabernacle. Olaudah Equiano was buried here, as were two of Karl's children.

In front of you is busy Tottenham Court Road. This was the arena of one of the most famous of Marx's drinking sprees. He was with the philosopher Edgar Bauer and the founder of German social democracy, Wilhelm Liebknecht. They decided to have a drink in every pub on Tottenham Court Road. 18 beers later, the German philosophers nearly got into a fight with a group of English Freemasons. They continued the evening by smashing street lamps and being chased through the streets of Fitzrovia by the police.

Turn right down Tottenham Court Road and then left into Great Russell Street until you reach the entrance to the British Museum.

Stop 15

This was Marx's second home for 30 years. It was where he studied and wrote the books that would influence future generations and change the world. They were real labours of love; the first volume of Capital had taken nearly 20 years. His publisher was promised two more volumes within a year of the first one. The publisher was disappointed, the two books remained unfinished at Marx's death 17 years later.

We are about to leave Marx, the philosopher, but there's another site opposite the museum which reveals a different side to this extraordinary family. At no. 55 Great Russell Street, the English premiere of the Doll's House by Henryk Ibsen was performed. It was a reading in Eleanor's front room. She had learnt Norwegian specifically in order to translate Ibsen; Eleanor took the female lead and George Bernard Shaw, the male.

AND FINALLY

You're very close to Tottenham Court Road Station. There are lots of great pubs around, especially in Fitzrovia. However, you have ended up opposite the Museum Tavern. This pub goes back at least 250 years and used to be called the Dog and Duck. The enterprising owner changed its name once he realised the British Museum was here to stay. Undoubtedly, Karl and Eleanor would have raised a glass or two many times in the bar, and it's as good a place as any to salute the memory of this pair of revolutionaries.

FURTHER EXCURSIONS

After completing the walk, it's a short trip up the Northern Line from Tottenham Court Road to Highgate Cemetery to see both the original, simple grave of Karl Marx and the grandiose monument erected to him and where Jenny, Eleanor and Helene Delmuth are also interred.

See **www.highgatecemetery.org** for opening times etc.

Also interesting is the Marx Memorial Library in Clerkenwell Square. Marx never went there but it became the headquarters of the Social Democratic Federation, the first Marxist political party in Britain. Lenin worked there in 1902, and in the library, you can see the small room where he edited Iskra, the Russian revolutionary paper. It's only open a few hours each week. Next door is the Crown where it is said Lenin and Stalin enjoyed a pint after a hard day's agitating. If you want to go to the library, see **www.marx-memorial-library.org.uk**

8. BAZALGETTE AND THE TRANSFORMATION OF LONDON

INTRODUCTION

Joseph Bazalgette, 1819-1891, was one of the great engineers of Victorian London. He truly transformed the city, and life, for its inhabitants. One of his obituarists claimed that he saved more lives than any other Victorian public servant, while another said he had added 20 years to the life expectancy of the typical Londoner. Yet today, his name is not widely known and he has only a somewhat neglected monument on the Embankment. He deserves to be much better remembered.

So who was he? His grandfather was a French Huguenot or Protestant fleeing religious persecution; his father became wealthy and Joseph studied engineering. He became chief engineer for London's Metropolitan Board of Works, in other words he became responsible for the development of the infrastructure of London for over 30 years. It is no exaggeration to say that he transformed London in the second half of the 19th century. Amongst some of his achievements were the commissioning and building of the Blackwall Tunnel, Northumberland Avenue, Leicester Square, Shaftesbury Avenue and Charing Cross Road; the rebuilding of Battersea, Hammersmith and Putney Bridges; the creation of Battersea Park and the building of the Blackwall Tunnel. Under his schemes, some 40,000 people were moved from the slums into newly built houses. But his greatest achievement was something much more profound and far-reaching: the creation of London's modern sewage system. This really was revolutionary; it ended the scourge of cholera and other water-borne diseases which killed thousands of Londoners every year.

In the first half of the 19th century, London was experiencing exponential growth. In 50 years, the population grew by around 250%. One of the consequences of this growth was that it put the existing sewage disposal system under great strain. At the beginning of the century, it had worked tolerably well. Most houses had a cesspit in the cellar which was supposed to be emptied regularly by the night soil men. The poo was then taken off to be spread on the fields surrounding London. Of course, this didn't always work well; Pepys often complained about the overflow from his neighbour's cellar which then flooded his own house with excrement. The sewers that existed, some from Roman times, were used only for dealing with rain water.

Indeed, it was illegal to use them for sewage. But the system was beginning to break down. There were a number of reasons:

Firstly, night soil men were beginning to go out of business; the fields were getting further and further away as London expanded and the market for human manure declined as fertiliser from South America was cheaper and more productive.

Secondly, medical 'science' was leading experts down a blind alley. Thinking at the time centred on the 'miasma' theory, in other words, that air, and the smells in the air, had dramatic effects on the human body. One commentator even wrote: *'From inhaling the odour of beef, the butcher's wife obtains her obesity'.* More to the point, if there was a bad smell, disease would follow. It was a very wide-spread idea, and accepted as common sense. Florence Nightingale went to her deathbed in 1910 believing in the theory. So miasma was the accepted explanation for the terrible diseases that ravaged London at the time, such as typhoid and cholera. What this implied was that if you cured the smell, you cured the disease. Given that cesspits were very, very smelly, they were seen as the cause of infection. Of course, they often could be when their contents leaked into the water supply. But it wasn't the smell that killed, it was germs in the water. And there was a great new invention which seemed to cure bad smells – the water closet. Thomas Crapper's factory in Kings Road (it existed there until 1966) spread the news with the catchy slogan: *'A certain flush with every pull.'* A WC seemed a godsend but suddenly you had an awful lot of water and only a little bit of waste. You couldn't put that in a cesspit. So in 1815, new houses were allowed to use the existing sewers for poo and by 1848 all new houses had to use them. But all sewers led to the Thames. Once the excrement ended up in the Thames it just stayed there, floating back and forth gently in the tide.

Suddenly, the Thames became an open sewer. Salmon stocks vanished. The water became a deep, dark brown and stank, especially in the summer. It was a disaster waiting to happen.

By 1850, the Thames was in a catastrophic state. Both Charles Dickens and Michael Faraday wrote to the Times of the awful condition of the Thames. One commentator wrote: *'The flood ... is now, below London Bridge, bad as poetical descriptions of the Stygian Lake, ... where are ye, ye civil engineers? Ye can remove mountains, bridge seas and fill rivers. Can ye not purify the Thames and so render your own city habitable?'*

Meanwhile, the cesspits underneath the older parts of London were full to overflowing as the population increased. In poor areas with over-crowding, itinerant tenants and unscrupulous landlords, often no one took responsibility for keeping the cesspits clean, and then they leaked into the water supply. This contributed to a mortality rate of 50% in children under 5. The problems became even more acute with the arrival of cholera in 1831 when 6,000 Londoners died. In 1848, a further 14,000 perished from this terrible disease while five years later, another 10,000 died.

Things came to a head in 1858 with the Great Stink. A hot summer led to intolerable conditions along the Thames. Parliament was forced to shut down so awful was the stench. Remember also that the MPs thought their lives were in danger as they breathed the dreadful 'miasma.' Something had to be done. The MPs commissioned Joseph Bazalgette to start work. The initiative was a great centralising project in the management of London, leading to the creation of the Metropolitan Board of Works and eventually to a London-wide government. The old system of government by parish just couldn't cope with a massive project for the whole of London.

So Bazalgette was in charge of designing and implementing one of the greatest British engineering projects of all time. North of the Thames he built three great sewers from Hampstead, Paddington and Hammersmith. They all met at Abbey Mills near Barking, 10 miles or so downstream from the city. This was mirrored south of the river with three sewers running from Putney, Clapham and Dulwich. They met at Deptford and then the main sewer ran down to Crossness in Abbey Wood. The pumping stations at Abbey Mills and Crossness were beautifully decorated with wrought-iron pillars and ceramic tiles. Their function was more mundane: when the sewage arrived in East London it was pumped into the Thames at high tide so the current would take it out to sea.

This was perhaps the greatest building project London had ever seen. 85 miles of main sewers were built across central London. 165 miles of existing sewers were refurbished, and 1100 new sewers were built. Every sewer, every connection, every element of the project was supervised and approved by Bazalgette. Along the way, the sewers had to overcome London's hidden rivers, its new underground railways, its canals and the undulations of London's geography. All this was accomplished in less than seven years.

The consequences of Bazalgette's project were revolutionary. Outbreaks of cholera came to an end once the new sewers were put in place. The Thames became much cleaner, moving from being the filthiest to the cleanest great metropolitan river in the world within a decade.

Bazalgette's scheme is still at the very heart of London's sewers 150 years later. Of course, there were a few modifications. The dumping of raw waste in the Thames at Barking came to an end after 20 years after complaints from East Londoners, and the terrible Princess Alice tragedy, when perhaps 700 passengers died in the sewage when a pleasure cruiser sank. After that, the poo was laden into boats and dumped in the North Sea for the Belgians to worry about. That continued until 1998 when Britain was forced to discontinue the practice. (We now seem to have revived this old tradition with the current government allowing water companies to merrily dump excrement in the nearest river or beach.) But Bazalgette's system proved robust enough to serve London well; only now, is there a need for another super-sewer along the Thames to relieve the burden on the existing system.

Perhaps the greatest visible legacy of Bazalgette's work was the creation of three embankments along the Thames through central London. They were the Albert Embankment, running for a mile along the south bank from Westminster Bridge to Vauxhall; the Victoria Embankment, stretching from Blackfriars to Westminster; and the Chelsea Embankment from Battersea Bridge to Chelsea Hospital.

These embankments had multiple uses. Primarily they were to hold the great sewers beneath the streets, but the Victoria Embankment was also used to take trains of the District Line underground railway. They also created some 80 acres of new land for London. St Thomas's Hospital, recently made homeless by the building of the railways, was relocated to the Albert Embankment. They also provided a very valuable flood defence protecting low-lying areas like Vauxhall and Chelsea from high tides. Most immediately, they provided new roads to ease the chronic Victorian traffic jams, especially along the Strand. It's along these embankments that our walk will take us.

FURTHER READING

The Great Stink of London, by Stephen Halliday, is a really good read.

8. Bazalgette and the Transformation of London   109

THE WALK

We will walk along all three of Bazalgette's Embankments. It's quite a long way and so I'd recommend doing the walk in two sections: perhaps from Embankment Tube to Pimlico. Then, from there, you can walk to Chelsea and perhaps on to Battersea Power Station. You can, of course, bail out at a number of different points or split it into more sections.

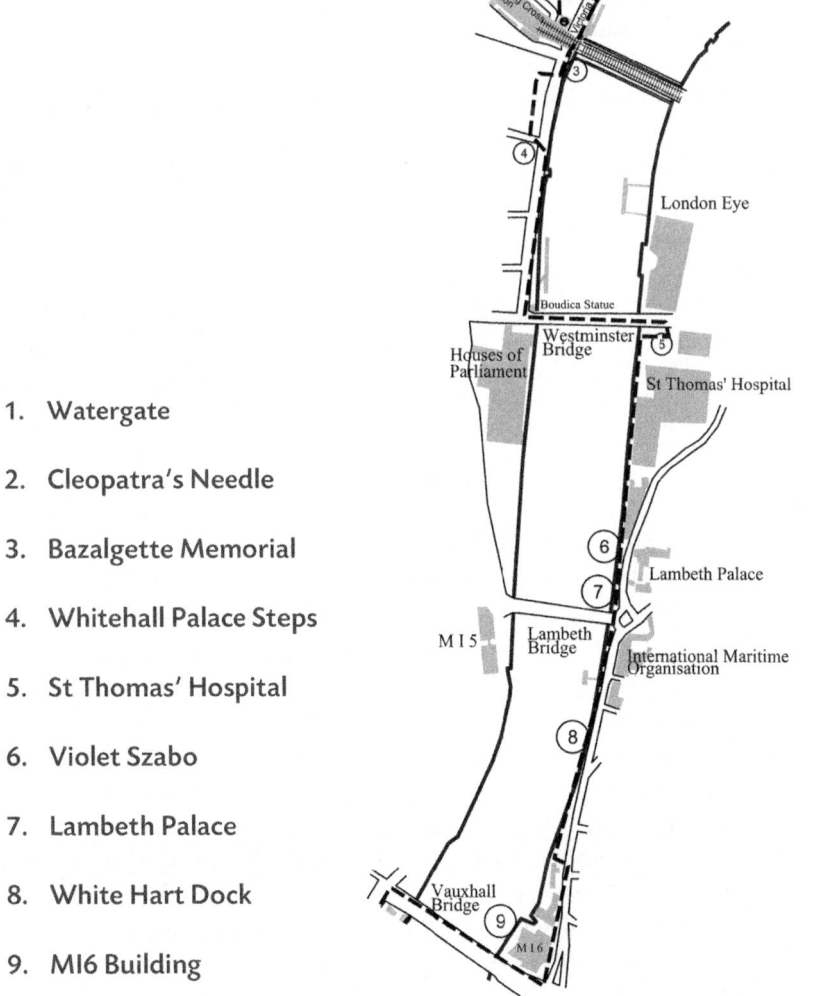

1. Watergate

2. Cleopatra's Needle

3. Bazalgette Memorial

4. Whitehall Palace Steps

5. St Thomas' Hospital

6. Violet Szabo

7. Lambeth Palace

8. White Hart Dock

9. MI6 Building

THE ROUTE

We start, fittingly, at Embankment Tube where we probably arrive on the District or Circle Line. This is very appropriate, as the trains are using the Victoria Embankment in the same construction of Bazalgette, which houses the great Northern Outflow. As you speed along in your train, so the poo is speeding along towards Barking.

Turn into Villiers Street and then right into Victoria Embankment Gardens. In front of you there is one of the very few water gates left in central London.

Stop 1

This is the York Watergate and dates from the 1620's. It marked the river entrance to the Duke of Buckingham's great house, which stood behind it in what is now Buckingham Street. Passengers would arrive by boat and then walk up the stairs behind. The gate is now marooned 150 yards from the river, and this simple fact shows the scale of the Bazalgette project.

Walk to the left of the café and cross the busy road to arrive at Cleopatra's Needle overlooking the river.

Stop 2

This has nothing to do with Cleopatra, as it was carved 1400 years before she was born. It had been given to the British in 1819 by the Egyptian ruler, but only transported to London, and erected nearly 60 years later. At its base is a plaque commemorating the seamen who died transporting the enormous column. Look around and you'll see the Egyptian theme continued on the benches lining the Embankment. This was one of the great showpieces of Victorian engineering and little expense was spared in beautifying it. This was supposed to be town planning for a city at the centre of the greatest empire the world had ever seen and it needed decorations to match. Look at the ornate lamp posts which bear sea monsters and the initials of the Metropolitan Board of Works of which Bazalgette was chief engineer. The Embankment became the first street to be lit by electricity in 1878, although the system adopted proved unreliable and it reverted to gas lighting until the 20th century.

Walk along the Embankment, under the railway bridge, and immediately you come to the Bazalgette Memorial on the Embankment wall.

Stop 3

Bazalgette deserves much more than this somewhat grubby memorial to him. His bewhiskered face peers out of what is meant to be a cross section of the sewer. It bears the words *'Flumini Vincula Posuit'*, loosely translated as *'He placed chains on the river.'* Poor Joseph is not well known; one of his descendants, Peter Bazalgette, is probably more famous for creating Big Brother and Deal or No Deal, leading to the somewhat unfair jibe that both Bazalgettes were made famous by excrement.

Opposite the memorial is Northumberland Avenue, also built by Bazalgette to give access to the new road. This was lined with offices and hotels and sold by the government to try and recoup some of the expenditure in building the system.

Cross over the Embankment and walk through the gardens crossing Horse Guards Avenue. On the corner, look over the wall to see another old river entrance.

Stop 4

These are the river steps to the old Whitehall Palace. The ones you see were designed by Sir Christopher Wren after a fire had destroyed much of the old medieval palace. However, a second fire led to the palace being abandoned by William III and redeveloped, first as private housing, and later as state offices.

Carry on walking through the gardens of Victoria Embankment, scattered with statues and memorials, mainly of a military nature. This is appropriate given we are walking behind the Ministry of Defence. The fact that they are here at all is due to an unlikely hero, W H Smith MP, of the stationery firm. Gladstone, the great Liberal prime minister, wanted to build offices to offset, costs but Smith fought the proposals and eventually Gladstone backed down.

Cross over the Embankment towards the statue of Boudicca (now defending the city she once utterly destroyed) and then cross Westminster Bridge to treat yourself to the classic view of the Houses of Parliament. Try and imagine the scene, and perhaps the smell, of the summer of 1858, with the river bubbling away below you and great sheets soaked in lime across the windows of Parliament to try and purify the air.

Cross Westminster Bridge. It's painted green while Lambeth Bridge upstream is painted red. Why? Because the Commons has green benches and is closest to Westminster Bridge, while the Lords has red leather benches and is at the Lambeth Bridge end.

Walk to the end of the Bridge then turn right into the garden of St. Thomas' Hospital.

Stop 5

This is one of the great institutions of London. It was described as ancient in 1215, so has been serving South London for well over 800 years, and perhaps centuries longer. Originally based in Borough High Street, Guys' Hospital was built next to St. Thomas' in 1721 to provide for the 'incurables' discharged from the former. But St. Thomas' had to move in 1871 when it was compulsorily purchased to make way for the expansion of London Bridge Railway Station. It needed a lot of new land, and where better than the area reclaimed from the river by Bazalgette. This is the start of the Albert Embankment, and from here to Lambeth Palace, you're walking on reclaimed land.

In the hospital is the Museum devoted to Florence Nightingale. She was a nurse here and founded the nurse training school at the hospital in 1860, the first secular school in the world. International Nursing Day is held every year on her birthday. There is a memorial to another great nurse in the garden, Mary Seacole, a woman of colour from Jamaica who also served in the Crimea.

Retrace your steps out of the garden and then walk down the Embankment, following the wall that is now a memorial to all those who died in the Covid pandemic. The red hearts commemorating the dead seem to stretch for ever.

There are fine views behind you to the Houses of Parliament.

Eventually the wall ends and there is a small green in front of you with a statue in the middle.

Stop 6

This commemorates the Special Operations Europe, one of the secret services of the British Government, set up in the Second World War. Agents were sent into occupied Europe to work with the local resistance movements; 117 of them died. The bust is of Violet Szabo who represents all those agents. She was a 23 year old mother who flew into occupied France twice but was captured, tortured and executed in Ravensbruck Concentration camp.

The site is a fitting one as close by are the headquarters of both MI5 and MI6.

Continue walking down the Albert Embankment for another few yards until you reach, on your left, the entrance to Lambeth Palace.

Stop 7

This was where the grand opening of the Albert Embankment took place in 1869, where the great and good assembled to celebrate the transformation of the south bank of the Thames. The Palace is the London residence of the Archbishop of Canterbury. It first became his home around 1200, but most of what's left is 14th and 15th century, while the internal buildings were heavily remodelled by the Victorians.

Continue to walk along the Embankment. A statue of a boat, sticking out of a modern office block, tells you that you're walking past the headquarters of the International Maritime Organisation. While across the river, the two white buildings with a great arch between them are the headquarters of MI5.

As you walk past the corner of Black Prince Road, you'll see on your left a strange construction of skeletal boats with seats looking as if they're made of boats' prows. This is White Hart Dock.

Stop 8

It's worth having a look at the dock, not because it's particularly beautiful, but because it shows some of the challenges that Bazalgette had to deal with when building the Embankment. Before Bazalgette, this was a tidal, low-lying area where many small firms were based. The building of the Embankment cut these firms off from the river, potentially putting them out of business. To give them access to the river, docks were cut into the bank so at high tide their produce could be floated into the Thames. Almost all of these docks have long since disappeared, but a very few remain, and this is one of them.

Keep walking along the Embankment. Soon you come to the hulking mass of the MI6 building.

Stop 9

This is one of the more controversial buildings in London. It was designed by Terry Farrell in his distinctive post-modernist style. Apparently based on an Aztec temple, it has been called a variety of names, including Babylon on Thames and Ceausescu Towers. It has been regularly attacked, and sometimes destroyed, in recent James Bond films. Currently, because of building work for the new super sewer, you're forced inland, but hopefully the Thames Path will be restored once work has finished

8. Bazalgette and the Transformation of London

and you're able to get to Vauxhall Bridge along the river.

Cross the Thames at Vauxhall Bridge. We've walked for over three miles, so this may be a convenient place to break the walk, as Pimlico Station is only about 400 yards away down Bessborough Gardens and then to the left.

Otherwise, turn sharp left at the end of the Bridge and down some steps to find our way back on to the Embankment, continuing to walk west. We walk through modern riverside developments with views of the high rise blocks of Wandsworth. Warning: these developments are private so the gates may be locked against you. Normally, however, you can stick next to the river.

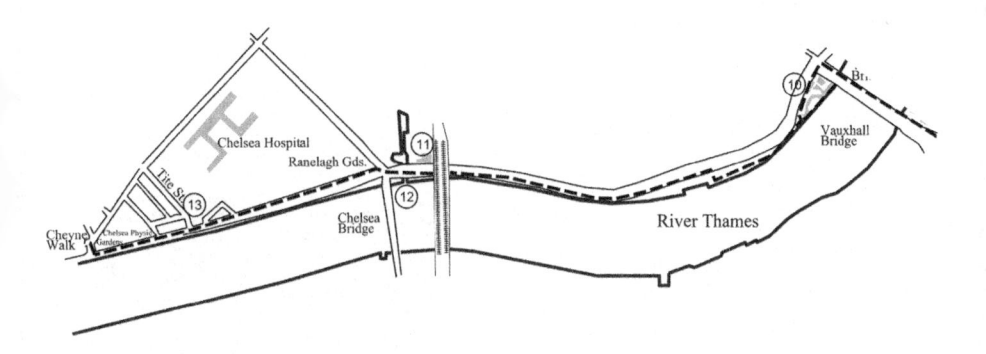

10. River Tyburn Outflow

11. Pumping Station

12. Grosvenor Canal

13. Tite Street

Stop 10

Shortly, you come across a plaque on the river wall marking the outfall of the river Tyburn. This is one of London's lost rivers, which had been long covered over, but still flowed under the city's streets. Bazalgette used their flow to flush his new sewers and keep the waste flowing east. As a result, the Tyburn's flow is now much smaller than in the past, except in very wet conditions. When that happens, the flood can force raw sewage into the Thames, which is what the new super-sewer is designed to stop.

Keep walking along the private pathway. Eventually you reach Pimlico Gardens with its statue of William Huskisson, a pretty obscure politician from the 1820's. He's dressed as a heroic Roman statesman, but his main claim to fame is that he was the first railway fatality. He managed to get run over by Robert Stephenson's pioneering locomotive, Rocket, on its opening run.

You're now forced on to Grosvenor Road and you keep walking westwards. On your right is Dolphin Square, once the largest self-contained block of flats in Europe. Given its proximity to Westminster, it has always attracted politicians. At one time there were 70 MPs and 10 Lords living there. Other residents were Christine Keeler and Princess Anne as well as plenty of spies from MI5 and MI6. Sometimes the spies were Russian-employed, like John Vassall, who also lived here.

Keep walking along Grosvenor Road until you reach the railway lines running over the road into Victoria Station. On the far side of the tracks, on your right, is the Great Western Pumping Station.

Stop 11

What this building did, and still does, is to pump 55 million gallons of sewage a day up 18 foot in order to get a slide on down to Barking. Our sewage flows using gravity. Without pumping, the slope would be so gradual that the system would not function. Every so often along its route to the east, the sewage has to be raised so it can continue to flow.

Keep walking and, within 100 yards, walk down some stairs to your right as you come to an inlet which at hightide is full of water.

Stop 12

This is the Grosvenor Canal. Opened in 1824, it used to run for about ¾ mile inland. Originally, water from here was supplied to west Londoners as drinking water, until the practice was banned in 1852. Later, it was used to import coal into the area and finally, for many years, it was used to export the rubbish of Pimlico. Its length was greatly diminished by the building of Victoria Station and now it serves as a water feature for the posh flats all around. You can walk over the swing bridge and then rejoin Grosvenor Road once more.

You have come to Chelsea Bridge and if you're tired out after around 5 miles of walking, you could pick up a bus from here to Sloane Square or walk over the river and pick up a Thames Clipper from Battersea Power Station Pier. You could even visit the refurbished Battersea Power Station, which some people seem to like, and then take the Northern Line from there.

To finish the walk though, carry on along the road, which is now called the Chelsea Embankment. You pass first Ranelagh Gardens, home of the 18th century pleasure gardens where Mozart played and Casanova courted. Then comes the Chelsea Hospital, one of Christopher Wren's greatest buildings, and home to the red-coated pensioners.

Very soon you pass on your right, Tite Street.

Stop 13

Artistically, this is one of the most notable streets in Britain, but it only came about because of the building of the Embankment by Bazalgette. Indeed, it's named after a member of the Metropolitan Board of Works, the body responsible for building the Chelsea Embankment. Once the land had been reclaimed, it became a prime residential area close to the river, but also close to the lights of the West End.

As you walk up the street, you notice that some of the houses have enormous windows. This is because they were built as, or converted into, artists' studios. From around 1880, some of the most notable artists in Britain lived and worked here. These included James McNeill Whistler, Augustus John, John Singer Sargent and the author and wit, Oscar Wilde. There are plaques to the last two in the street.

Return to the Embankment and continue to walk past the beautiful late 19th century houses. You pass the Chelsea Physic Garden set up by the Guild of Apothecaries 250 years ago.

You've arrived at Cheyne Gardens, now separated from the river by Bazalgette's Embankment, with its fine gardens. It's a very desirable place to live and residents have included: at no. 3 Keith Richards, no. 4 George Elliot, no.13 Vaughan Williams, no.16 Dante Gabriel Rossetti and no. 21 was another home of Whistler.

At the end of the block, look out for a plaque announcing that this was the site of Henry VIII's Manor House. This is a remnant of a time long before Bazalgette, where the rich escaped the squalor of the city and went to a place where the water was clean and the air fresh. We have Bazalgette to thank for restoring the Thames to something how it used to be.

AND FINALLY

There are some interesting pubs nearby. There's a proper pub, the Prince Albert, just over Albert Bridge by Battersea Park. On our side of the river there's the Cross Keys, very much a gastro pub but which claims Whistler, Sargent, JMW Turner and Bob Marley amongst its past customers.

The nicest way to get back to central London is by getting on a Thames Clipper from nearby Cadogan Pier. Otherwise, you could take the bus along the Embankment to Victoria.

OTHER EXCURSIONS

If you're still wanting to walk, you could carry on along Cheyne Walk, past Chelsea Old Church with its memorials to Sir and Saint Thomas More, who lived nearby. You'll pass Crosby Hall, an original medieval merchant's house moved from Bishopsgate to Chelsea in 1910. You could even carry on to West Brompton Cemetery where, among others, Emmeline Pankhurst, is buried. You'll be close to Fulham Broadway tube.

If you want to stick with Bazalgette, you could go for a stroll down Northumberland Avenue, Charing Cross Road and Shaftesbury Avenue, as it was his planning that built these three roads and transformed the West End.

9. THE LAMMINS OF ORCHARD PLACE

This walk takes us to an unknown area of London but with some of the capital's most spectacular views. There are some well-known names along the way; the most famous by far is Michael Faraday, the discoverer of electro-magnetism. But I am going to concentrate on one extended family, the Lammins, who lived in our area 150 years ago. They're not famous at all, but perhaps they can represent the millions of nameless poor who have populated London over the centuries. The names of these ordinary Londoners are rarely commemorated so, in this book, let the Lammins stand for those we have forgotten.

The area through which we are walking is between Blackwall, to the east of the Isle of Dogs and Canning Town, where the River Lea flows into the Thames. Here the Lea meanders through East London, forming a double S bend and creating two islands, almost completely surrounded by water. This is Orchard Place. It was, and is, very isolated. Cut off from the rest of London for hundreds of years, there was only one track that linked this area to civilisation in the form of Poplar.

Because it was so isolated and so dominated by the Thames and the Lea, it was the perfect place to set up the noxious, polluting, space-demanding industries of Victorian London. The prevailing westerly winds blew the fumes out to sea, or at least into Essex, while the tidal river acted as a gigantic sewer, taking pollution away from London. As a result, the area became a centre for all the industry that the city did not want within its borders. Much of the employment in the area was based around the river. In particular, the great East India Docks dominated the area. They were built in 1806 to service the East India Company which was, at that time, importing a flood of goods from the colonies in the East. The imports were then transported down the East India Dock Road, specially built through East London, to provide a safe passage to the great warehouses in Cutler Street.

Around these docks other industries were developing. Part of the riverside was taken over by Trinity House, an institution founded by Henry VIII to look after inland navigation including harbours, lighthouses and naval charts. In Victorian times, Trinity Buoy Wharf, as it is now known, became its main workshop where buoys were repaired and new models developed. It was also where experiments were carried out to make sure lighthouses were as efficient as possible and new lighting techniques introduced. At its peak, some 150 men were employed here. One of them was Michael Faraday who was employed as an electrical engineer on the design of lighthouses and on ways of combatting corrosion.

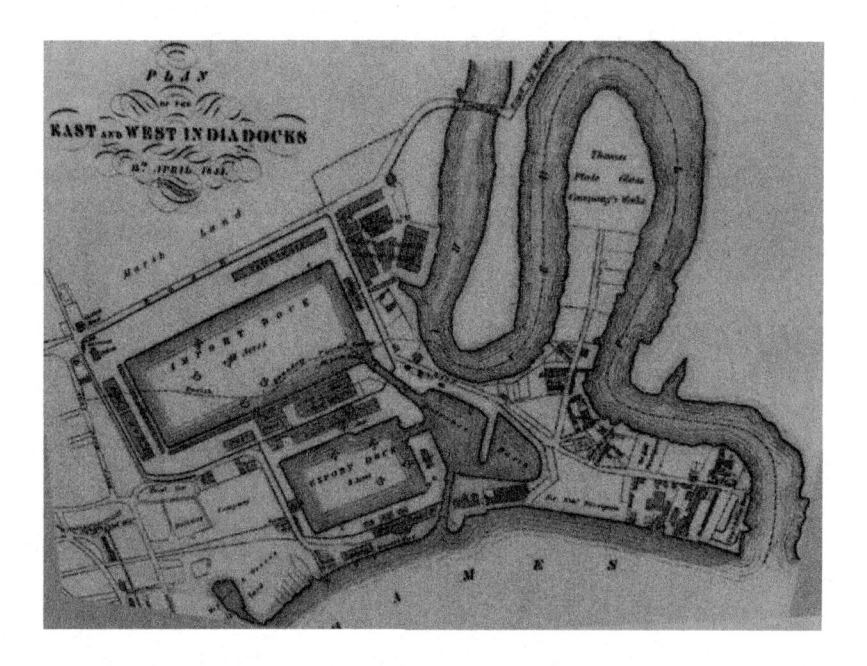

Another major industry was ship-building. London was a major shipbuilding area right up until the eve of the First World War. Great firms were based here, such as the Samuda Brothers, Ditchburn and Mare and, most famously, Thames Ironworks and Shipbuilding Company Ltd. The latter built the world's first all-iron warship, HMS Warrior, in 1860. (It still exists and is moored in Portsmouth Harbour.) The company continued to build ships here for another 50 years, including the great Dreadnoughts, built to maintain Britain's naval sea power. The last one was HMS Thunderer, launched in 1911. Its construction marked the end of an era as it was the last Royal Navy ship to be built on the Thames. Thames Ironworks, under its chairman Arnold Hills, saw itself as a model employer to its 5,000 or so employees. It was one of the first to introduce an 8-hour day for the workers when 10, or even 12 hours a day, was quite typical. He also helped create a works football team for his employees. Thames Ironworks FC changed its name after five years to West Ham United FC and that's why the football club still sports two riveting hammers on its crest.

Another key industry in the area was food processing. Perhaps the most famous was the processing of whale meat. The first factory rendered down blubber to extract whale oil. It was set up by James Mather in the 1790's. A typical entrepreneur of the time, he was involved in whaling, slave-trading and transporting convicts to Australia. His whale rendering didn't last much more than a decade but whale meat was still being processed for food in this area late into the 1930's.

Another company was the Thames Plate Glass Company which, in the middle of the 19th century, was probably the biggest employer on the island. Nearly half the employees were women, employed because of the 'superior delicacy of their touch' in polishing the glass. The factory produced glass for very high-quality telescopic lenses and exhibited its products at the Great Exhibition of 1851. It closed in 1873 because of competition from the USA and many of those employed by the glassmakers eventually emigrated to Indiana to continue to work in the industry. Part of the factory was then taken over by the Blackwall Galvanised Iron Company which kept going into the 1970's.

The total population of Orchard Place would probably have been in the mid hundreds in the 19th century, while many thousands more workers would have commuted into the area. Those few hundred soon gained a very bad reputation. There were four pubs in the area but for many years no church. There was *'neither a butcher, baker, barber, post office, police station, fire station or pawn shop or tram or bus'* but only a couple of houses selling the most basic of provisions. To get out of the area you had to walk for two miles down a dark and deserted street to Poplar.

Social commentators bemoaned the fact that the inhabitants were *'rough, poor, piratical and predatory.'* Charles Booth reported that *'the law as ordinarily understood hardly runs in Orchard Place and a policeman is very rarely seen.'* A local clergyman, Father Lawless, called them *'hardly human'* and *'incarnate mushrooms'* adding that *'God must have made a mistake incarnating them.'* A very Christian view.

This was an isolated, inward-looking community with early marriage *'often at 16 or 17 and generally for very pressing reasons.'* Overcrowding was rife; Charles Booth reported that just five houses sent 57 children to the local school. Over the years, the area became dominated by a handful of very large families, so much so that in 1930 it was reported that 100 of 160 children at the local school were called Lammin. Because of their poor reputation local people tended not to be employed by the large firms in the area. Instead, the inhabitants scratched a living from the river, often doing odd jobs such as cleaning ships' boilers, unloading barges or simply scavenging on the banks of the Thames. The one bright spot in this deprivation was probably the local school. It received good reports from local inspectors and had an innovative curriculum, including ensuring that all the children were taught to swim. This was a life preserving skill as the Lea and Thames were the children's playground and later their workplace.

One of the nicknames for Orchard Place was Bog Island. It lay just a few feet above high water mark and flooding was a regular occurrence. Things reached a head in the Great Flood of 1928 when the whole island flooded. In 1931 the Evening Standard declared it *'London's Lost Village'* and the London County Council rehoused most of the population onto the 'mainland' in Oban House in Poplar a few hundred yards away. The old sub-standard accommodation was knocked down and Orchard Place sank into decline for 80 years.

Today the area is the site of extraordinary redevelopment. The island itself is now dominated by modern blocks of housing with some 800 new homes. Transport has been revolutionised with the Jubilee Line and the DLR opening up links to central London and Docklands for the first time. Some major cultural institutions have been established there, most noticeably the training school for the English National Ballet. The Lammins would definitely not recognise the place. But they were here first and deserve to be remembered.

FURTHER READING

I have not been able to find a book to recommend on this subject. There are some monographs about the area and the London Borough of Tower Hamlets has an excellent resource base on the area.

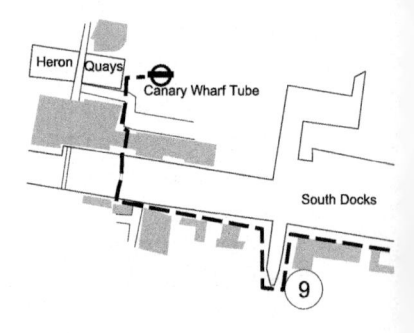

THE WALK

The walk can be exposed along the river, so best to pick a fine day, especially when the tide is full. You'll be rewarded with wonderful views.

1. Canning Town Station
2. Bow Creek
3. Orchard Place
4. Trinity Wharf
5. Trinity Buoy
6. East India Dock
7. Virginia Settlers Monument
8. Coldharbour Lane
9. West India Docks

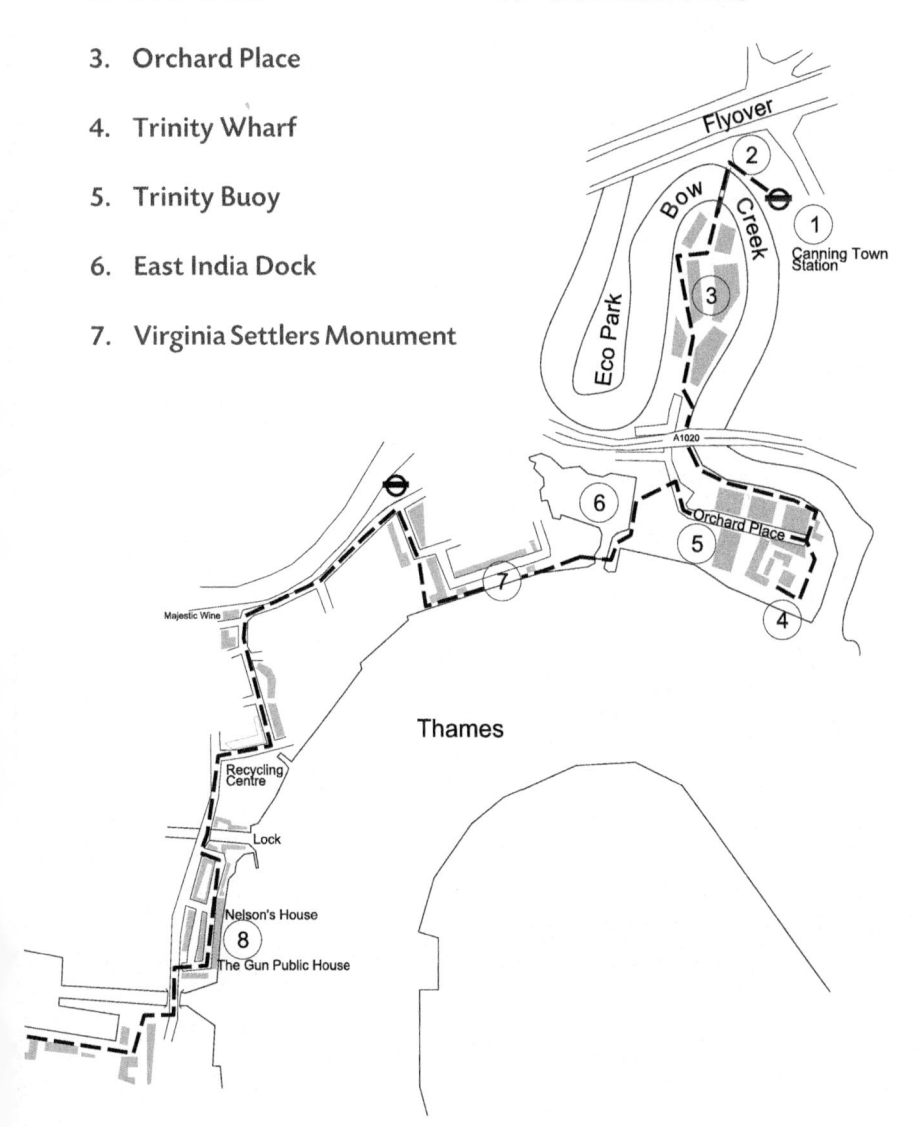

THE ROUTE

This is a beautiful walk along the Thames with great views of the redevelopment of the last 30 years. But we will try and imagine life in the 19th century when this area was at the heart of industrial London and where the wealth of the city was being created.

Stop 1

We start at Canning Town Station. At the ticket barriers, exit to the right and go up the escalators. At the end of the entrance hall there is a memorial to the Thames Iron Works in the form of a panel from HMS Warrior, one of the first great battleships built in the yard. It's an immediate reminder of the industrial heritage of the area we are about to explore.

Go back through the station, past the ticket barriers and ascend to ground level using the lift or stairs. You're now standing on the banks of the River Lea or, as it's called here, Bow Creek.

Stop 2

The River Lea is, historically, one of the great boundaries of London. In medieval times its power was harnessed to drive mills and so it became a centre for early industry. Over the years, its position downstream and downwind of London meant that all the noxious, smelly and polluting industries tended to locate to the east, and the Lea's function as a readymade sewer meant that waste could be disposed of cheaply, if not safely, into the river.

The Lea can be a very confusing river. For a start its name varies from the River Lea to the Lee Valley Park and Lee Navigation. As it nears London, it's been canalised and there are a number of different courses with interlinking channels and you're never quite sure if you're looking at the main channel. Where we are standing now, there is a great double loop in the river which has formed an S bend leading to the formation of two peninsulas almost entirely surrounded by water. The first is Bow Creek Ecology Park, a surprisingly peaceful and occasionally beautiful place amid what was once probably the most polluted part of London. If you want to visit the park, simply follow the riverside path round to the right and in a few hundred yards you'll find yourself surrounded by nature.

Otherwise, cross over the footbridge and enter Orchard Place.

Stop 3

Orchard Place was once one of the most isolated communities in London and yet it was the home to some very significant industries. During the 19th century it was home to whale rendering, gas works, galvanised iron works and glass works. These have now been replaced by the cultural industries of the 21st century, including the English National Ballet training facility. As you stand facing the ballet school, the plate glass works would have once stretched right across the peninsula in front of you. Later it became the site of the island's school with its surfeit of Lammins. A bit beyond, on the right hand side, was the 'Ocean Harvest' factory which canned whale meat.

Walk through the Island, veering along the right hand bank. This gives you views over the Creek to the nature reserve beyond.

At the end of the Island, go under the flyover and walk straight on along Orchard Place. At a sign for Samuda Bros, shipbuilders from the 1840's, turn left and walk along the river bank.

As you walk along, try and imagine the scene from 150 years ago. On the opposite bank would have been the great shipbuilding centre of the Thames Iron Works, where thousands of men were employed, making the great ironclads that were at the heart of British naval power. Today, it is very different with gulls and grebes feeding on the mud flats. After a few hundred yards, the river path ends and you walk right, then left, to arrive at Trinity Buoy wharf.

Stop 4

Trinity Buoy Wharf is truly one of the most remarkable spots in London. It has stupendous views across the Thames to the Dome and Canary Wharf. What's also remarkable is the industrial, artistic and scientific work that has taken place here.

There is so much of interest in this spit of land. On your left, there's a café with a taxi on the roof and a tree growing out of the chassis. Next to it, you will see a Lighthouse Ship, now a recording studio. On your right, there is the Electrical Store dating back to the 1830's. As you walk round you will see London's only lighthouse. This was an experimental laboratory where Trinity House could try out improved forms of illumination. Today it houses the Longplayer, the millennial project, where a composition is due to play till the year 3000 without repetition. The music is played on Tibetan bowls and gongs and the whole project was devised by Jem Finer, a member of The Pogues. NB Currently, this is open only at the weekends. At its foot is possibly the world's smallest museum, housed in a garden shed. It is dedicated to Michael Faraday, who was employed here to develop better lighting for lighthouses. Faraday, although mainly self-educated, was the father of the electromagnetic industry. Everything we take for granted, from mobile phones to underground trains, rely on his discoveries.

The wharf has now become a cultural and crafts centre housed either in historic buildings or in brightly painted containers. All around you can be seen statues, iron sculptures or other offerings from the artists' workshops. It's a great place just to wander round and watch the river flow.

When you've seen all that Trinity Buoy Wharf has to offer, and perhaps had some refreshment at the quirky café, walk back down Orchard Place until you reach an enormous buoy in the road.

Stop 5

The buoy represents the work of Trinity House and around it are signs for the industries that are now long gone. They include Samuda Bros, Thames Iron Works and Mare Ltd, all shipbuilders along with Mathers Whale Oil. Unfortunately, the signs are not original; it would be remarkable if they were given the time they're commemorating, often over 150 years ago, and the amount of development and change that has taken place. But not to worry: they are reminders of a forgotten and hidden past and for that I, for one, am grateful.

Continue along Orchard Place until you reach some iron gates on your left which lead into the East India Docks Basin.

Stop 6

In front of you is a large basin which is gradually silting up to form a nature reserve, attracting a range of wildfowl including, if the signs are to be believed, kingfishers and teal. This used to be the holding basin of the East India Docks where the great ships waited to sail on the tide for India and the East. This was the smallest of the three dock basins. In front of you, to the right, is the entrance to the channel of the import dock, while to the left of there is the exit from the smaller export dock. Unfortunately, both the import and export docks have been filled in and redeveloped. The dimensions of these docks were once enormous. The total area was 36 acres, roughly 24 football pitches, and they could handle up to 250 ships at a time. They were 30 feet deep and all this earth was shifted with pick, shovel and barrow.

We walk round to our left and cross over the lock gates and walk along the riverbank. In a few hundred yards we come to our next stop, the Virginia Monument.

Stop 7

The Virginia Monument commemorates the early settlers who left from here in 1607 to found Jamestown, the first permanent English settlement in North America. It made sense to leave from here rather than near the city as the ships didn't have to traverse the great loop of the Isle of Dogs.

Continue walking along the river and turn right inland along the meridian line as the riverside path ends. Walk through the small estate and then left along the road, Blackwall Way. You're walking around the site of the old Blackwall Yard which boasts a history of shipbuilding dating back to the 17th century. You pass on your right a Majestic Warehouse which 150 years ago was a hydraulic pump station for the railway that served the docks. Keep straight over the mini roundabout along Blackwall Way towards the recycling centre at the bottom of the road. (I promise you it does get better.)

Bear right at the bottom and then you meet Preston's Road which goes right round the Isle of Dogs. Walk along the road to your left and cross a bridge over the first entrance to the West India Docks.

When you reach Coldharbour turn left, and you enter a very different world from the bustle of the traffic and the views of Canary Wharf.

Stop 8

Suddenly the street is cobbled and quiet and just on your left is a house called Nelson House because, according to legend, the great naval hero used to live there. Unfortunately, it's almost certainly untrue. The house probably dates from around 1820 and Nelson was dead by then. It's more likely that he lived on an earlier house on the site.

A little bit further up the road is one of the great pubs of London: The Gun. Named after the ceremonial cannon, which opened the West India Docks, there's been a pub here for around 300 years. It's a wonderful place with great views across the river from the balcony. It claims that Nelson used to meet Lady Emma Hamilton there for secret assignations in an upstairs room

Walk away from the Gun back on to Preston's Road and turn left. Cross over the Blue Bridge. This is the main entrance for the West India Docks and is still in use.

Immediately after the bridge, take care crossing the road and drop down the steps opposite to walk along the South Dock of the West India Docks. Soon a channel interrupts your progress and this is a good place to pause to admire the dimensions of the docks.

Stop 9

You're now standing in the middle of the West India Dock complex. The body of water facing you is the export dock. Through the channel to the north you can glimpse the Import Dock while at your back another channel leads southward to the Millwall Dock. If we thought the East India Docks were big, the West India Docks are enormous. They are almost three times the size of the East India Docks with 90 acres of water. Their dimensions have been narrowed in the last 30 years or so as the demand for building land in the docklands has encroached onto the basins.

Walk south to cross the channel and then walk back to continue westwards along the dockside to pass over the footbridge.

Cut through the building in front of you and you will see the various stations for Canary Wharf where our walk ends.

AND FINALLY

Canary Wharf is awash with cafés, bars and restaurants, although the best pub, by far, is The Gun, which we passed 20 minutes ago.

FURTHER EXCURSIONS

If you are in Canary Wharf and are interested in the docks then you really must visit the Museum of London Docklands, **www.museumoflondon.org**. It is one of the great London museums and both comprehensive and accessible on all things to do with the history of the docks. It's a 10 minute walk on the other side of Canary Wharf.

10. THE SUFFRAGETTES: FROM OUTSIDERS TO WESTMINSTER

The suffragette movement in the years before the First World War was, and remains, one of the greatest episodes in the fight for equal rights that London has ever seen. The movement, led by Emmeline and Christabel Pankhurst for the right of women to vote, was extremely controversial and hard fought, leading to an extraordinary level of violence on both sides.

The demand for women's equality can trace its roots back certainly to Mary Wollstonecraft's *'Vindication of the Rights of Women'* published in 1792. However, the organised movement for Women's Suffrage really began with the petition that John Stuart Mill and Henry Fawcett presented to Parliament in 1866 on behalf of a group of women. The petition was rejected but the movement spread. 30 years later, the National Union of Women's Suffrage Societies was created which brought together all the local organisations. It was led by one of the great figures of the suffrage movement: Millicent Garrett Fawcett, Henry's widow.

By the early years of the 20th century, many of the activists in the suffragist movement were increasingly frustrated by its slow progress. There had been limited gains: some women could stand and vote in school board elections for instance. But pressure was building for more rapid change fuelled by more radical methods and in 1903 Emmeline Pankhurst founded the Women's Social and Political Union in her house in Manchester. Emmeline had been involved in the suffragist movement since the 1880s and was closely allied to the emerging Labour Party. She and her three daughters, Christabel, Sylvia and Adela, were well-known in socialist circles and knew, for instance, Eleanor Marx, George Bernard Shaw and Keir Hardie. Disillusioned by the lack of progress, Emmeline set up what we would now call a single issue campaign.

The WSPU was to be open to women only and had no party political affiliations. Its sole purpose was to gain votes for women on the same basis as men. This was a highly contentious position. At the turn of the 20th century there was a property qualification for voting and it is estimated that only 60% of men were able to vote. So rather than campaigning for universal adult suffrage, the WSPU was campaigning for the rights of middle class women. This put them at odds with those women and men in the emerging Labour Party who wanted universal adult suffrage.

The WSPU's motto was 'Deeds not Words', something they rapidly put into effect. The WSPU took to the streets, organising demonstrations and rallies across the country. The focus was often on Westminster where the WSPU and other groups would present petitions, lobby ministers and try to force their way into Parliament. By June 1908 the WSPU was able to organise a women's march on Parliament which attracted as many as 250,000 people.

Within this mass movement the WSPU was not a major force, at least in terms of numbers. At its peak it had perhaps only 5,000 members. Compare this to the National Union of Women's Suffrage Societies which had around 50,000. But what the WSPU did have was a genius for publicity. A Daily Mail journalist called this new, radical movement the *'Suffragettes'* in an attempt to mock and diminish them. (Think pigs and piglets!) But the WSPU adopted the name with pride, distinguishing themselves from the more gradualist suffragists, by saying the SuffraGETtes would GET women's suffrage done.

The WSPU was completely dominated by Emmeline and Christabel Pankhurst and astonishingly undemocratic. Emmeline's conception of the movement was that 'The WSPU is simply a suffrage army in the field' and army discipline was needed. In 1907, at its conference, a draft constitution for the movement was theatrically ripped up and trampled underfoot by Emmeline. Annual conferences were abolished and decisions were taken by a council appointed by Emmeline. Any member who criticised or even questioned policies was expelled. This led to a succession of splits and expulsions from the WSPU. The most important was probably in 1907 when many leading suffragists, such as Charlotte Despard, split to form the Women's Freedom League which rapidly became an important voice in the suffrage movement.

Over the next few years the tactics of the WSPU continued to escalate in the face of government intransigence. Women chained themselves to railings and were arrested, sometimes violently. A Ju-Jitsu team called The Bodyguard was set up to protect the leadership, and those being arrested, from the police. A radical wing to the movement, The Young Hot Bloods, a group of younger, more militant women, emerged which was at the forefront of the more controversial tactics of the WSPU.

By 1912, the WSPU had embarked on a national campaign of militancy. Stone throwing campaigns were launched where hundreds of windows were broken in central London and across Britain. Many women were being imprisoned, sometimes hundreds in a single day. The arrested suffragettes, denied political prisoner status, began to go on hunger strike. Sylvia, for instance, was arrested eight times in 18 months, undertaking a hunger strike each time. At first, women were force fed, a brutal procedure. The authorities, frightened of the publicity that would accompany a high profile death, introduced the *'Cat and Mouse Act'*. This was where imprisoned women on hunger strike were released for a week or so in order to regain their strength before being re-imprisoned.

The suffragettes' tactics became yet more extreme. Paintings were slashed, pillar boxes were set on fire and bombs were placed in politicians' homes, railway stations and sports stadiums. 32 churches, including Westminster Abbey, were bombed. Railway signal wires were cut with the intention of causing accidents. At least five people died in the bombing campaign and dozens more, often postal workers, were injured. There were casualties amongst the suffragettes too: one suffragette bomber died and Emily Davison was killed at the Epsom Derby trying to pin a scarf on the King's horse. That it was a terrorist campaign was acknowledged by Christabel and Emmeline who published a weekly column called 'The Reign of Terror' in their newspaper. Most later historians of the movement agreed with that assessment.

At the time the campaign of violence was very controversial even amongst leading members of the WSPU. The problem was that such tactics, by definition, were individualistic and secretive. It relied on a small number of very committed women taking extraordinary risks to promote the cause. It did not involve the great mass of ordinary women and men in any kind of activity. Indeed, some of their activities were almost bound to alienate many potential supporters of women's suffrage. Alternative strategies, such as working with the Labour Party, which by now was committed to universal adult suffrage or campaigning for wider social reform, were discouraged. As a result, the WSPU was always in the headlines but was losing support and members.

Emmeline and Christabel ruled the movement with an iron first. Opponents or dissidents were summarily expelled. Even two of Emmeline's daughters, Adela and Sylvia, were expelled. Sylvia was thrown out in 1914 for working too closely with the Labour Party in the East End of London. She too had objected to the campaign which relied on individualistic acts of violence. Poor Adela was simply given a one-way ticket to Australia. She never saw her family again.

As a result of these controversies, the WSPU was seen by many as becoming less and less relevant to the political movements of the day. They were increasingly isolated and their militancy was becoming ever more extreme. One of Christabel's backers wrote to her thus: *'People are now saying that from the leader of a great movement you are developing into the ringleader of a little rebel Rump.'*

And then the First World War came. Immediately, Emmeline and Christabel threw themselves behind the war effort and became amongst the most extreme of patriots denouncing pacifists, trade unionists and conscientious objectors as either fools or German agents. Their paper was renamed 'Britannia' and spoke little about the right to vote, concentrating on the reporting of the war effort. The two became active participants in the 'White Feather' campaign which tried to shame those men not in uniform to enlist. The WSPU had further splits as members rebelled against the Pankhursts' new direction. Finally, the WSPU disbanded itself and re-emerged after the war as 'The Women's Party'. By then, a new franchise law had been passed. All men over 21 were allowed to vote while women had to be over 30 and own some property either directly or through their husbands. Christabel stood as the only candidate for the Women's Party but was defeated and the movement was wound up. Christabel moved to California and in 1926 Emmeline joined the Conservative Party, a long way from her radical roots. She died in 1928 just a few months before the law was passed giving women the same voting rights as men.

The suffragette campaign raises all sorts of questions relevant to today's world. We look back on them now as heroines of the struggle for women's rights. Statues are erected, police bands play and plaques unveiled. It seems that the end did justify the means. I wonder if we'll extend the same latitude to, say, the climate activists of today.

FURTHER READING

There are many books about the Pankhursts, the WSPU and the fight for Women's Suffrage.

A single volume that I found interesting is: *The Pankhursts,* by Martin Pugh.

This examines not just the political activities of the WSPU and the Pankhursts, it also looks at the sometimes tortured relationships between them.

Walking with Londoners

THE WALK

Our walk takes us through the heart of the West End passing where the suffragettes organised, demonstrated, slashed paintings, smashed windows, laid bombs, were arrested and where, after their victory, they were commemorated. This walk is a bit longer than some of the other walks so you may want to split it in two. A convenient stopping place would be in Covent Garden between stop 7 and 8.

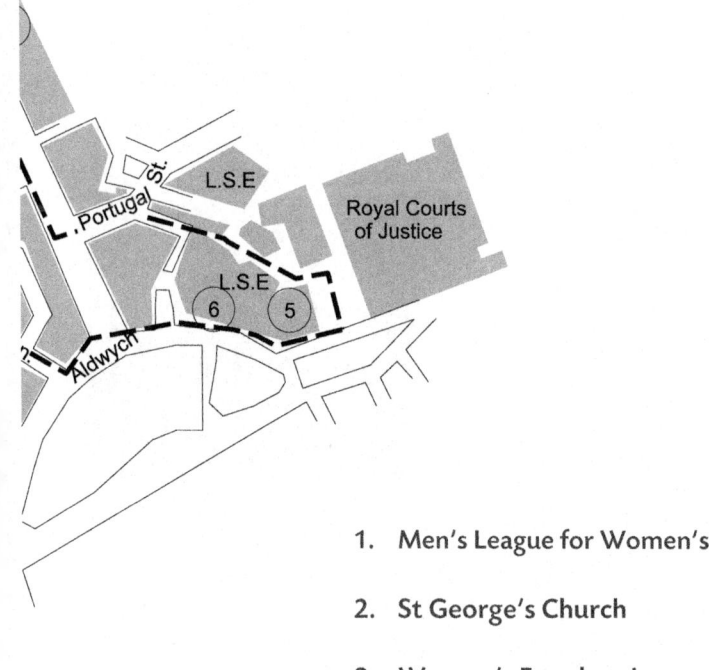

1. Men's League for Women's Suffrage HQ
2. St George's Church
3. Women's Freedom League HQ
4. WSPU HQ
5. Pethick-Lawrence House
6. Aldwych Skating Rink
7. Bow Street Museum
8. Trafalgar Square

THE ROUTE

We start at Tottenham Court Road Station and walk down New Oxford Street, bearing left into Bloomsbury Way. Immediately on your left, turn into Museum Street and stop outside no. 40.

Stop 1
This was the home of the 'Men's League for Women's Suffrage'. It was founded in 1907 by a group of (male) academics and intellectuals to support the women only WSPU. Bertrand Russell, who lived just round the corner, stood unsuccessfully as a suffragist candidate backed by the group in its early years.

Retrace your steps and turn left along Bloomsbury Way until you reach St. Georges' Church.

Stop 2
Unfortunately, this Hawksmoor church is often closed but do go inside if you can as it is very beautiful. It has a remarkable steeple with lions and unicorns, representing England and Scotland, fighting at its base surmounted by George I who is bringing peace to the combatants. In our story it is notable for being where the funeral service for Emily Wilding Davison was held after her death at the 1913 Derby. Thousands of suffragettes accompanied her coffin to Kings Cross Station where it was transported to Morpeth in Northumberland for burial.

Cross Bloomsbury Way and turn right down Bury Place to the corner of Barter Street.

Stop 3
Here you'll find a plaque to the Women's Freedom League whose headquarters were nearby. The Women's Freedom League split from the WSPU in 1907 after the Pankhursts brought the organisation under their complete personal control and turned it to increasingly violent tactics. The WFL were seen as militant; their

members chained themselves to public buildings, disrupted meetings and were sent to prison (and force-fed) for non-payment of taxes. They refused, however, to join in the violence that was associated with the WSPU. The WFL also worked closely with the emerging Labour Party who had committed themselves to universal suffrage. The WFL were a very influential voice with more branches and followers than the WSPU, especially outside of London. Their leaders included Charlotte Despard, Edith How and Teresa Billington. Ada Salter, who we meet in the last chapter, was also a prominent supporter.

Go along Barter Street and turn right at Southampton Place, left down High Holborn. At the lights cross diagonally to Holborn tube and walk south down Kingsway.

Stop 4

On your left you soon come to 42 Kingsway. Lincoln's Inn House is now luxury accommodation but it once housed the headquarters of the WSPU. It was raided many times by the police, most notably on 13 April 1913 after Lloyd George's house had been bombed and partially destroyed.

Keep walking down Kingsway and turn left into Portugal Street, then right down Clare Market and into Clement's Inn.

Stop 5

When this area was redeveloped by the London School of Economics, it became the site of the Women's Library with its resource centre relating to the suffrage movement. There's a small exhibition of suffragette photos in the windows and the offices are named after important fighters for women's suffrage. It was also the site of the home of Emmeline and Frederick Pethick Lawrence, key supporters of the WSPU. They used their wealth to support and subsidise the activities of the WSPU including the costs of the suffragette newspaper. Frederick used his funds to bail out hundreds of arrested suffragettes (including his own wife). The couple used their home as a hospital for women to recover after being force fed or who'd been on hunger strike. Both were arrested once the window smashing campaign started. Imprisoned for 9 months, both went on hunger strike and both were force fed. They were then successfully sued for the damage caused by the stoning campaign even though they hadn't agreed with it. The Pethick Lawrences were almost bankrupted by their support for the suffragette movement yet remained true to the cause. However, their views diverged with the Pankhursts', especially over the issue of violence, and they were expelled from the movement. Both went on to become leading members of the Labour Party and remained active politically until their deaths.

Close by was St. Clement's Press which published the Suffragette paper.

Carry on walking down the passage until you reach Aldwych near the Royal Courts of Justice. Turn to your right.

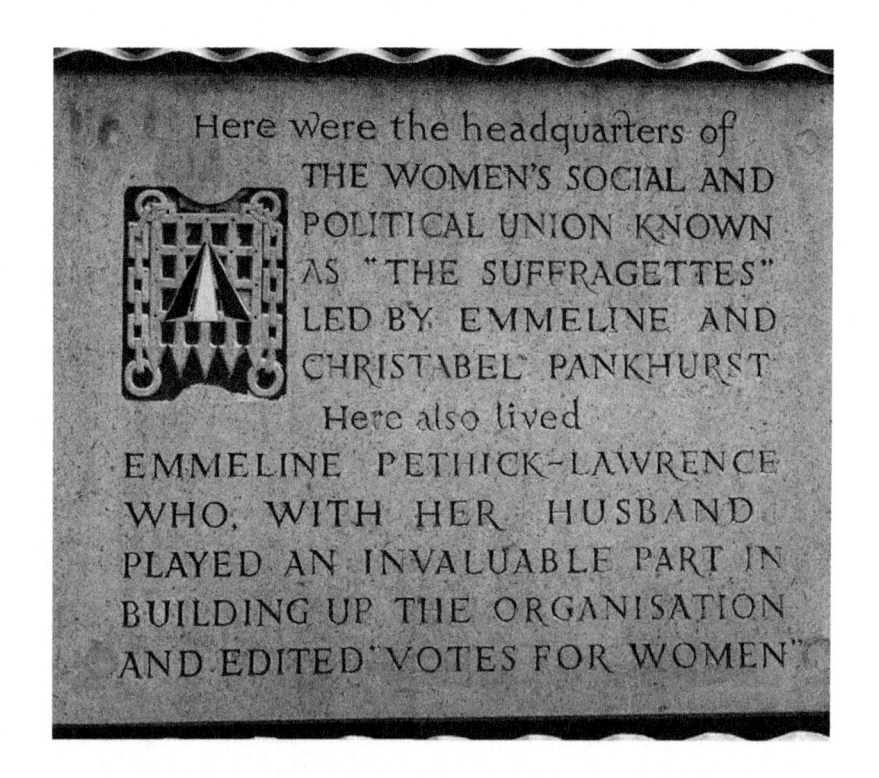

> Here were the headquarters of
> THE WOMEN'S SOCIAL AND
> POLITICAL UNION KNOWN
> AS "THE SUFFRAGETTES"
> LED BY EMMELINE AND
> CHRISTABEL PANKHURST
> Here also lived
> EMMELINE PETHICK-LAWRENCE
> WHO, WITH HER HUSBAND
> PLAYED AN INVALUABLE PART IN
> BUILDING UP THE ORGANISATION
> AND EDITED "VOTES FOR WOMEN"

Stop 6

This was the site of the Aldwych skating rink; the scene of mass civil disobedience by the suffragettes. On census night in 1911, hundreds of suffragettes packed into the rink in order to evade being counted: a small act but mighty irritating for the authorities.

Keep walking round Aldwych, cross Kingsway and then turn right up Drury Lane. Turn left into Russell Street and then right into Bow Street.

Stop 7

On your right is Bow Street Magistrates Court and a small Police Museum (with admission charge) which tells the story of the police from the Bow Street Runners, London's first professional police force, to the present day. You can also visit the actual cells where suffragettes were held after their arrest during the window smashing campaigns.

Carry on up Bow Street and turn left into Floral Street and walk down until you reach St. Martin's Lane and turn left.

You pass the monument to Edith Cavell, a British nurse shot by the German Army during the First World War. Her statue reminds us that many women in the suffrage movement were wanting not merely the vote but to play a much more active part in society than women were traditionally allowed. Many women in the suffrage movement joined in the war effort often in providing medical care to service men.

You arrive in Trafalgar Square.

Stop 8

This was the scene of much Suffragette activity, with the movement regularly holding mass rallies in the square. It was also the setting for more violent scenes. On 10 March 1914, Mary Richardson attacked Velasquez's Rokeby Venus, one of the most famous paintings in the world, in the National Gallery with a butcher's knife, inflicting terrible damage on the picture. The assailant earned the soubriquet of 'Slasher Mary' as a result. Three weeks later the suffragettes laid a bomb packed with nails in St Martin's in the Fields church. It blew out the windows of the church and showered passers-by with glass fragments.

9. Cannon Row

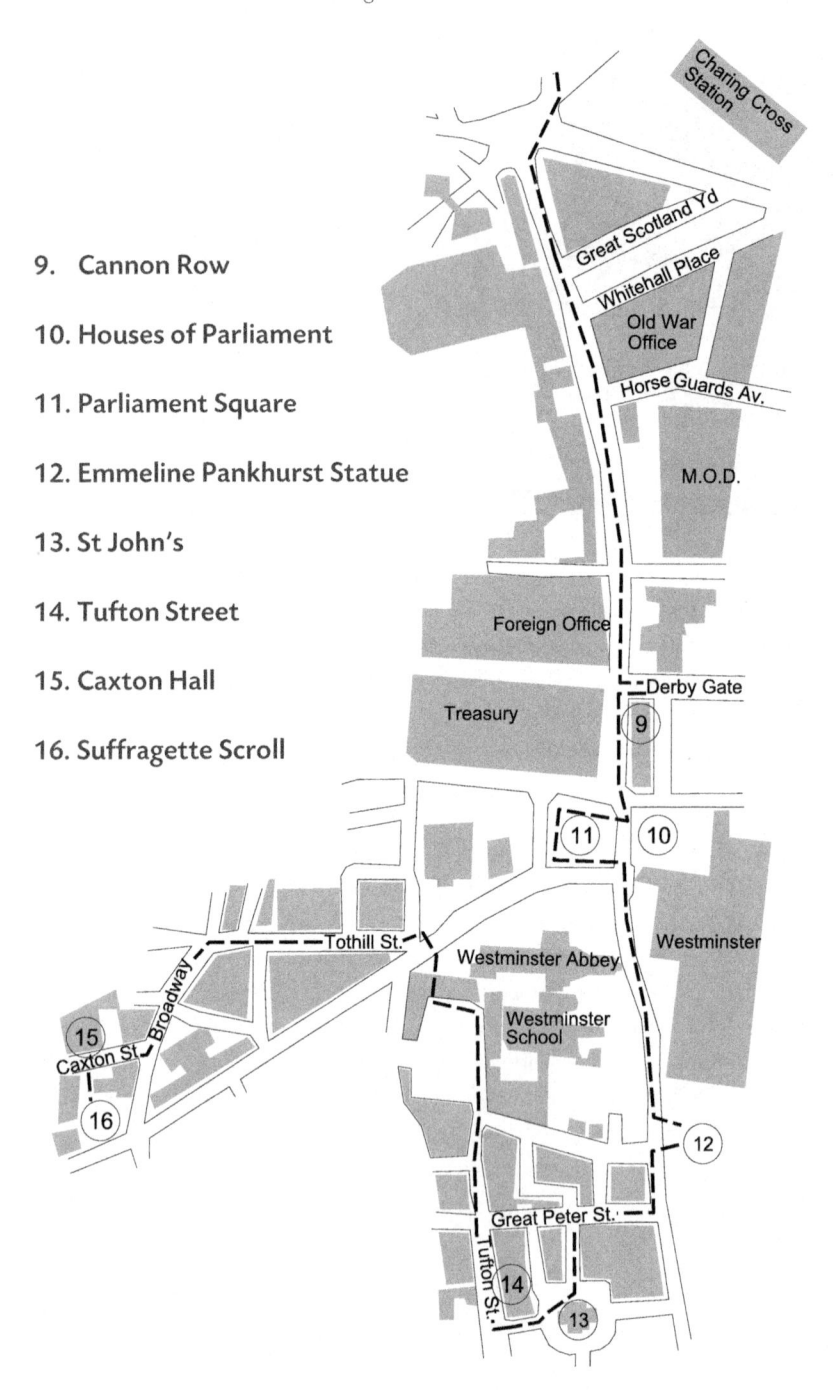

10. Houses of Parliament

11. Parliament Square

12. Emmeline Pankhurst Statue

13. St John's

14. Tufton Street

15. Caxton Hall

16. Suffragette Scroll

Leave the Square and walk down Whitehall. Go past Downing Street, remembering that two suffragettes posted themselves as parcels to No. 10 in an attempt to speak to Mr Asquith, the Prime Minister. They were turned away by staff but the two women made national headlines by their stunt.

Keep walking along Whitehall, then turn left into Derby Gate just after the Cenotaph.

Stop 9

In front of you is Cannon Row Police Station where women were taken after being arrested in demonstrations in Parliament Square or after demonstrating in the Houses of Parliament. Just about every nationally known leader of the WSPU, along with hundreds of other women, spent a night in the cells here. Today, it is still heavily guarded, but now provides accommodation rather than imprisonment for Members of Parliament. (At which point there are plenty of comments that can be made!)

Retrace your steps and continue walking along Whitehall until you reach the Houses of Parliament.

Stop 10

Parliament was the focus of much of the activities of the suffragettes with the lobbying of MPs and ministers.

In 1911, on census night, Emily Wilding Davison hid in a cupboard in the Palace of Westminster so that she could claim Parliament as her address. Her hiding place is now commemorated with a plaque detailing the event. Suffragettes were also responsible for smashing windows in Parliament, chaining themselves inside the Ladies Gallery and interrupting debates.

Walk into Parliament Square.

Stop 11

This was the site of many suffragette demonstrations. One of the most notorious was the so-called Black Friday demonstration of 18 November 1910 when 300 women marched on parliament. They were first manhandled by groups of men and then met by lines of police. The violence continued for six hours, often of a sexual nature. 115 women were arrested on that day. Given the controversy surrounding the event, in the end none of the women were charged but neither was there any investigation into police misconduct. Many historians believe that the events of the day helped propel the WSPU into a more militant phase of direct and violent action rather than the more traditional methods of protest.

Walk to the back of the square and there you will find the most recent memorial to the suffragist movement.

The statue of Millicent Fawcett stands in the middle of the back line of statues, gazing at the Palace of Westminster. Fawcett was one of the great women of the suffrage movement from its earliest days. She lived to see the rights of all adults to vote enshrined in law just before her death in 1929. Around the plinth are engravings of 59 women and four men who were key to the long fight for women's suffrage. These include all four Pankhursts, including Sylvia and Adela, Emily Wilding Davison, Charlotte Despard, George and Minnie Lansbury (who, with Sylvia, feature in the next chapter), Mary Macarthur (who we meet in the last walk in this book) and the Pethick-Lawrences.

Look across to Westminster Abbey. This was the scene of one of the last and most violent suffragette actions when, on 11 June 1914, a bomb was placed in Westminster Abbey, next to the Coronation Throne. It exploded, splitting the Stone of Scone and damaging the throne. It had been packed with nuts and bolts to act as shrapnel against anyone close by. Luckily, no one was killed or hurt, although it blew out windows and was loud enough for MPs in Parliament to come running over. What price for freedom?

Walk between the Houses of Parliament and Westminster Abbey. At the end of the building you come to Victoria Gardens on your left. Enter the park.

Stop 12

In front of you there is a statue to Emmeline Pankhurst. It was unveiled in 1930 shortly after her death. At the ceremony, the Metropolitan Police band played 'March of the Women', the anthem of the suffragettes. How ironic that the force which had been used to batter the suffragettes should then provide the music for the celebration of her life. The plaque to Christabel was added in 1958, but Sylvia is only represented by the badge she designed for the suffragette movement.

Come out of the park and continue walking along Millbank and then turn right along Great Peter Street. Turn left down Lord North Street. In front of you is an unusual looking church, St John's.

Stop 13

Today, St John's Smith Square is mainly known for its music concerts, but a hundred plus years ago, it was the site of another bomb attack by the suffragettes on 1 March 1914. But they were forgiven. Emmeline's funeral was held here in 1928 and she was buried in Brompton Cemetery.

Bear right around the church, then turn right into Dean Trench Street and then right into Tufton Street.

Stop 14

As you walk along Tufton Street you'll see a plaque to Eleanor Rathbone, a leading suffragist, but perhaps best known for her tireless and successful campaigning for family allowances. Across the road is the back of the Millicent Fawcett Hall which was the headquarters for the London Society for Women's Service. Just beyond is Mary Sumner House. She was the founder of the Mothers' Union in 1876. By the end of the century it had over 160,000 members. It was also anti-suffrage arguing that women should be content with their role within local government and the home.

Keep walking down Tufton Street and walk into the grounds of Westminster School, one of the oldest and most prestigious schools in the country. Young women have been allowed in, but to the sixth form only. Up until then, the hallowed precincts are reserved for boys only.

Walk through the gate at the far end of the square and cross Victoria Street to walk along Tothill Street to the left. Turn left when you reach Broadway and then turn right down Caxton Street. A few yards along Caxton Street is the façade of Caxton Hall.

Stop 15
Caxton Hall was used by the WSPU to hold their annual Women's Parliament to press their demands for representation. After their deliberations, the women would often march to Parliament to try to meet ministers and MPs. It was also the site of the Women's Exhibition in 1916, which brought together women's suffrage societies during the war. Opposite the Hall, which is now luxury flats, is the entrance to Christchurch Gardens. Walk through.

Stop 16
On your right you will see a monument in the shape of a scroll. This was commissioned by the Suffragette Fellowship in 1970 to commemorate *'the courage and perseverance of all those men and women who in the long struggle for votes for women, selflessly braved derision, opposition and ostracism, many enduring physical violence and suffering.'* This is our final stop and an appropriate place to end.

AND FINALLY

You're very close to St. James's Park Tube Station or Victoria Station; both are within a few hundred yards. There are a couple of good pubs nearby: The Feathers on Broadway, the Sanctuary House Hotel or the Blue Boar, both on Dacre Street.

OTHER EXCURSIONS

To visit the grave of Emmeline Pankhurst you need to go to Brompton Cemetery, a few stops west on the District Line, where there is a fine memorial to her. All her daughters are buried abroad: Christabel in California, Sylvia in Ethiopia and Adela in Australia. Emily Davison was buried in her home town of Morpeth, Northumberland.

The Museum of London (closed until 2026) has always had an interesting exhibition on the suffrage movement in London. Let's hope that it is reinstated in the new museum.

11. THE WOMEN OF BOW

This is an extraordinary walk through a small, almost unknown, part of the East End, but one which played a central role in the creation of the mass trade union movement and the Labour Party. It's a story of four remarkable women who between them formed an unbroken history of working for the rights of ordinary women and men. The four were Annie Besant, Eleanor Marx, Sylvia Pankhurst and Minnie Lansbury. Of course, they were not alone; behind them were hundreds and thousands of working class women and men engaged in these movements.

So who were they?

Our first extraordinary woman is Annie Besant. She was married at 20 to a clergyman. The marriage was a disaster despite her having two children within it. In her autobiography she wrote that she was completely unprepared for the role and she soon separated from her husband. As a result, she lost access to both her children. If the divorce was scandalous at the time, what she went on to do was even more so. She started to earn a living as a journalist, writing articles attacking the role of the church in laying down society's rules and for the freedom of women to divorce. She met and lived with Charles Bradlaugh, the leader of the Secular Society. Together, they published a book on birth control which was deemed immoral. At one stage it looked likely they would be imprisoned until both were released on a technicality. They became household names and arguments raged about the morality of their actions. Charles went on to become a Radical MP fighting for the cause of secularism in public life.

By now Annie was one of the most well-known and influential journalists in the country. In 1888 she wrote a sensational article entitled *'White Slavery in London'* about the conditions of the match workers in the Bryant and May factory in Bow. She wrote of the long hours, starvation pay and the appalling danger of the work. The match workers suffered from 'Phossy Jaw' caused by phosphorous used in the matches attacking the bones of the skull. She contrasted the conditions for the workers with the enormous profits being generated for the directors. The article caused a scandal.

The factory managers sacked those young women who, they thought, had spoken to Annie, and the rest of the workforce walked out on strike. Annie became the secretary of the strike committee and so the 'Match Girls' strike began.

It was all over within a week. The unrelenting bad publicity forced the firm to back down. Promises to improve conditions were made, pay was increased, fines were abolished and the Union of Women Matchmakers, with Annie as its secretary, was formed.

The effect on the East End was electrifying: a group of women and girls had forced one of the biggest employers to concede much better working conditions. If the women could do it – why couldn't the men? Unions had up until then been mainly for skilled male workers, now the unskilled could see a way out of their position at the bottom of the labour market. First to strike were the gas workers of the East End, and then came the mass Dock strike of 1889. The great general trade unions were born from these two disputes. Today the GMB can trace its roots to the Beckton Gas Strike while 'Unite the Union' is descended from the London Dock Strike.

Annie went on to more extraordinary adventures. She became an important figure in East London, being elected to the London School Board with the responsibility, as she wrote, *'for 763,680 children of London in my hands'* even though, because of her divorce, *'Christian bigotry robbed me of my little child.'* She became increasingly interested in the fight for Indian Independence and worked with Nehru and Gandhi. When she died, she was given the equivalent of a state funeral by the Indian Congress movement.

Her epitaph, and one she always followed, was *'Better remain silent, better not even think, if you are not prepared to act.'*

One of Annie's friends was Eleanor Marx, daughter of Karl, and she threw herself into the new unionism that was being born in the East End. She raised money for the Match Girls and within six months became a key organiser for the Gas Workers. She was a friend of Will Thorne who became the General Secretary for the Union. He'd left school at six and was functionally illiterate. Eleanor was at his side through the strike, writing his speeches and the rules of the new union. She became a full-time organiser for the Gas Workers Union and ended up on its national executive. She was also active in the great Dock Strike which followed in 1889 and which transformed labour relations in Britain. That strike led directly to the birth of what became the Transport and General Workers Union and is now Unite. One of the new union's key demands was for the 8-hour day, and Eleanor was also at the heart of this movement. She was a very well known orator, often speaking to hundreds of thousands of people at mass rallies. She was also part of the movement which led eventually to the formation of the Labour Party. She was a friend and drinking companion of Keir Hardie, its founding father, as well as many of the leading socialists of the day.

As a result, Eleanor knew the Pankhurst family, who were well known in radical circles. Sylvia Pankhurst, the daughter of Emmeline Pankhurst, remembered meeting Eleanor when she was a teenager. Sylvia went to London's Royal College of Art but became increasingly involved in the suffragette movement. She had a long and loving relationship with Keir Hardie and was closely involved with the emerging Labour and Union movement. One of the first Labour MPs was George Lansbury who was elected for Bow in 1910. In 1912, he resigned his seat to force a by-election on the issue of Women's Suffrage and Sylvia was drafted in to help campaign for him. George was narrowly defeated but Sylvia stayed on and set up the East London Federation of Suffragettes, which rapidly became a very significant movement in the East End. Her close political allies in this movement were the Lansbury family who were at the heart of the Labour organisations in the area. George and his sons ran a wood yard in Bow but they were also councillors, the MP, and sometimes mayor, for the local area.

Sylvia's views began to diverge from those of her mother and sister, who were the leaders of the national suffragette movement. The key differences were that Sylvia wanted a movement of women **and** men to campaign for **universal** adult suffrage, whereas her mother only wanted to extend the existing limited suffrage to middle class women. Given the poverty of the area, Sylvia also wanted to work on a wide range of social issues and not just that of the suffrage, while her mother was adamant that the fight for the vote was the single issue to fight on. She was also critical of the more extreme tactics of the suffragettes, such as bomb attacks, as these tended to be individualistic and divisive. These differences came to a head in 1913 when her sister, Christabel, expelled Sylvia from the national movement.

Sylvia was undeterred. She launched her own paper: 'The Women's Dreadnought' and organised mass demonstrations, rallies and meetings across Bow for universal adult suffrage. She was arrested and re-arrested 8 times in 18 months during 1913 and 1914 under the 'Cat and Mouse' laws. After each imprisonment, she would go on hunger strike until her declining health meant she was released, only to be re-arrested when she had regained her strength.

The outbreak of the First World War led to a final split in the suffragette movement. Emmeline and Christabel supported the war effort while Sylvia opposed it. In the early days, at least, the war was popular but it had a devastating impact in the East End, especially on the women left behind. With their men at the front, women struggled with a loss of income, child care and poverty. Sylvia threw herself into supporting these women.

With the help of hundreds of women and men across the borough, Sylvia set up workshops for women to get employment and wages, created nurseries and creches to look after children and cost-price restaurants to feed the hungry. She remained adamantly opposed to the war, a very unpopular position at the time, but her work in the area meant she retained many supporters. Her politics also changed. The Women's Dreadnought became 'The Worker's Dreadnought' and, at the end of the war, she joined the newly-formed Communist Party. Ironically, when the suffrage was extended to some women in 1918, Sylvia argued for a boycott of the elections arguing instead for the revolution. By now she was living with Silvio Corio, an Italian political exile. In 1924, she moved out of the East End and at the age of 45 had a child, Richard. She refused to marry Silvio and her mother, Emmeline, broke all ties with her and never spoke to her again.

Sylvia remained politically active all her life, supporting anti-imperialist movements in Ireland, India and finally Ethiopia. She became a friend of the emperor, Haile Selassie, and when she died she received a state funeral in Addis Ababa.

One of Sylvia's key supporters during the First World War was Minnie Lansbury. She had been born to Jewish immigrants in the Whitechapel ghetto. She went to the Jews' Free School in Spitalfields and became a teacher in the East End. She was a union activist arguing for equal pay for men and women teachers and joined the emerging Labour Party. There she met and married Edgar Lansbury, son of George. She became secretary of the East London Federation of Suffragettes, working closely with Sylvia, and was chair of the War Pensions Committee, fighting for the rights of wives and widows and injured servicemen.

At the end of the War, Minnie became an alderman on Poplar Borough Council under George Lansbury's mayorship. The new Poplar Council immediately started to improve the living conditions in the borough. Medical centres were introduced, new homes were built, free milk was delivered to children, public works were introduced to provide jobs for the unemployed and a generous minimum wage was introduced which was the same for men and women. Minnie was at the very heart of all these initiatives. But there was a problem. The local council was at the centre of efforts to improve local living standards and, of course, the poorest areas had the greatest need and the fewest resources. Yet there was no attempt to equalise the burden across rich and poor areas. Worse, all councils had to pay the same cross-London fees to the police, the water board and the London County Council. These rapidly rising fees would have tipped Poplar into bankruptcy, so the Council refused to pay. The government took them to court and when the councillors still refused to pay the whole council was sent to jail in September 1921; men to Brixton, Minnie and the other women to Holloway. They were imprisoned for 6 weeks but, as other Labour Councils in the East End adopted the same tactics as Poplar and protests continued to spread, the government capitulated. Minnie and the other councillors were released and the rating system was reformed.

Minnie was free but the stay in prison had badly weakened her health. The 'Spanish Flu' epidemic was still a major health hazard and on 1 January 1922 Minnie died. She was 32. Thousands followed her coffin at the funeral and her ashes were interred at the West Ham Jewish Cemetery.

The East End remained at the heart of Labour politics for the next 20 years. George Lansbury was re-elected to Parliament, became a government minister and then leader of the Labour Party. His successor was Clement Attlee, the great reforming Prime Minister, who had been Mayor of neighbouring Stepney.

A last footnote: After Minnie's death, Edgar eventually remarried and had a daughter who went on to become the great actor, Angela Lansbury.

FURTHER READING

You could try the following: *Annie Besant: An Autobiography, Eleanor Marx*, by Rachel Holmes; *Sylvia Pankhurst*, by Shirley Harrison; or *Minnie Lansbury*, by Janine Booth. Rosemary Taylor has written a number of books about the period such as *In Letters of Gold* and *Voices from History: East London Suffragettes*

THE WALK

On this walk we look at some of the main sites and monuments where these four women lived and organised, from the Match Girls Strike of 1888, to the Poplar Rates Strike of 1921.

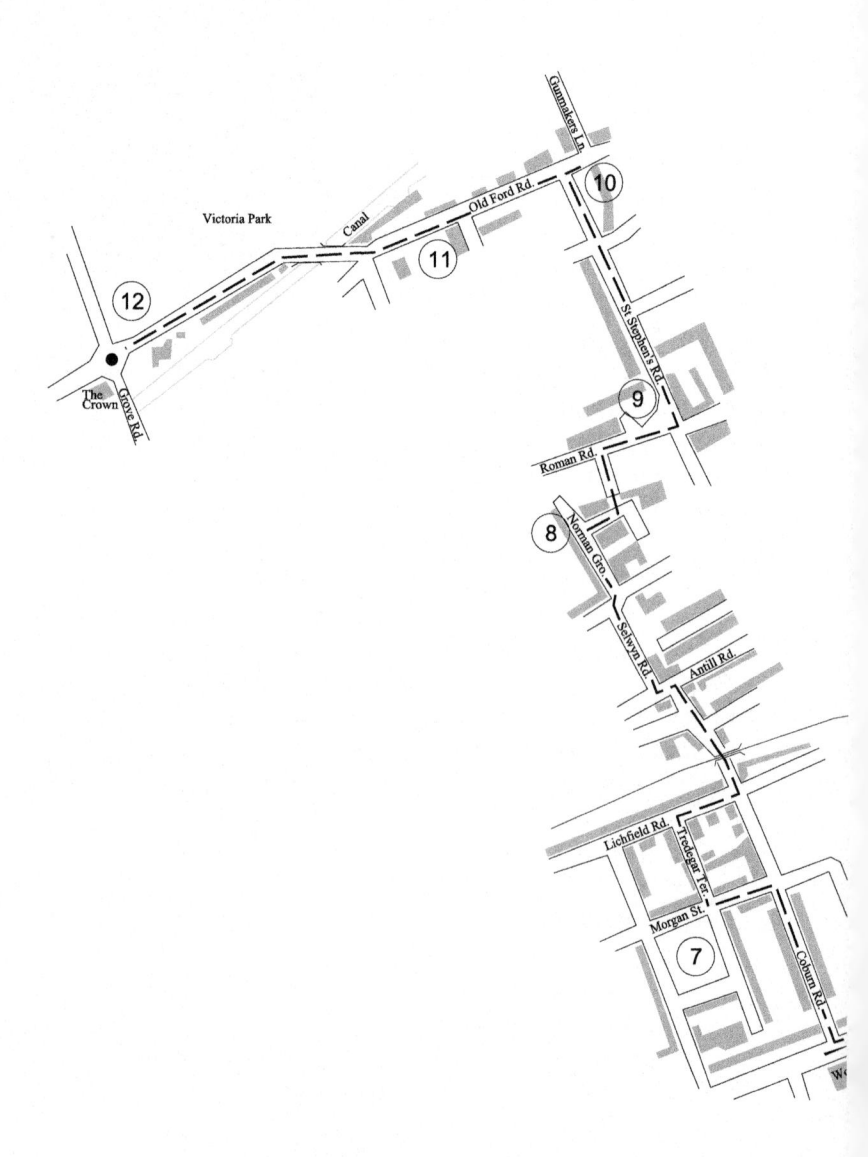

11. The Women of Bow

1. Bow Church
2. Match Factory
3. Poplar Town Hall
4. Bow Road Police Station
5. Minnie Lansbury Clock
6. George Lansbury House
7. Tredegar Square
8. Toy Factory
9. Roman Road
10. Mothers' Arms
11. Sylvia Pankhurst Mural
12. Victoria Park

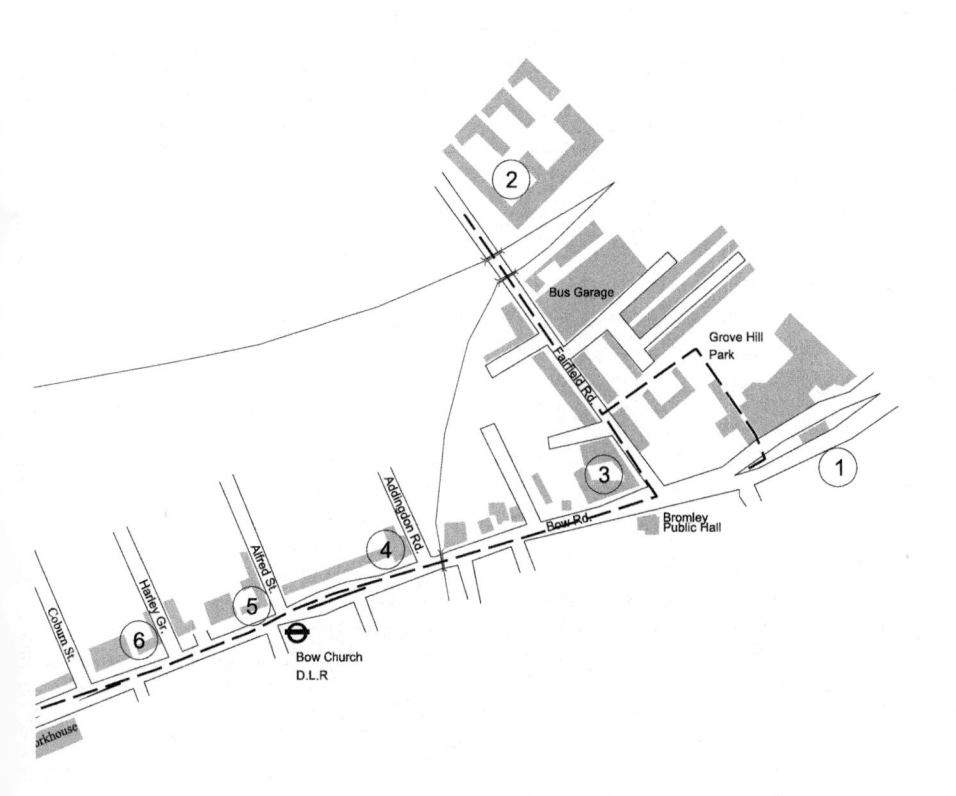

THE ROUTE

Our walk starts at Bow Church, close to the Docklands Light Railway Station or Bow Road on the Hammersmith and City and District lines.

Stop 1

We start at Bow Church, which is now surrounded by one of the busiest roads in East London. In the past though, it was a landmark on the Roman road to Colchester. Remarkably it has survived road-building, redevelopment and the blitz, with parts of the church dating back to the early 14th century. It has a bloody history; during the reign of Mary I many Protestants were burned outside the church.

Just outside the churchyard is an imposing statue of William Gladstone. The inscription is somewhat worn but you can just about read that it was donated by Theodore Bryant, owner of Bryant and May, in 1882. Now look at the statue's hands, they are painted red. The rumour had spread at the time that the match girls' wages had been docked to pay for the statue. They had certainly been given an unpaid 'holiday' to attend the unveiling. On the day, Annie Besant reported that: *'So furious were the girls ... that many went to the unveiling of the statue with stones and bricks in their pockets... A gruesome story is told that some cut their arms and let their blood trickle on the marble paid for, in very truth, by their blood.'*

There is now a tradition that the hands are painted and repainted red in memory of the match girls. Nobody seems entirely sure when the tradition began. Some say it started from the time of the Match Girls' Strike, while others say it started much later. Whenever it started, it still goes on. The hands were cleaned for the 2012 Olympics, the next day they had been repainted.

The first headquarters of Sylvia's East London Federation of Suffragettes was just to the south of Bow Church. The building has long gone but some similar buildings still exist on the north side of the road, and with heroic imagination, you can just about imagine Sylvia painting *'Votes for Women'* in letters of gold on her headquarters in 1912.

Walk through a small alley past the Nunnery Art Gallery, home to Bow Arts, and into Grove Hall Park. This was once a 'lunatic asylum', one of the largest in London. It also incorporates the garden of a Catholic convent which still operates on Bow Road. Walk through the park to Fairfield Road and turn right past the bus garage. It's called Fairfield as an annual fair was held in a field at the end of the road.

Stop 2

We soon arrive at the old Bryant and May factory. At its height, it was the biggest factory in London, employing over 3,000 women. Today it is the Bow Quarter, a gated development full of luxury flats with preposterous names like Manhattan, Lexington and Arlington. Look carefully and you will see the ark symbol of Bryant and May over the entrance. This is a site of enormous historical importance that deserves commemoration given it helped lead to the birth of 20th century Labour politics. Thankfully, it is marked by a blue plaque but, you may feel, deserves a great deal more.

Go back down Fairfield Road until you reach Bow Road again.

Stop 3
The white building on your right used to be Poplar Town Hall. If you look up by the entrance, you'll see a mosaic above your head detailing the docks and industries that once dominated the area. Opposite there is the imposing Bromley Public Hall. This was the scene of many of Sylvia's public meetings and many times she and her comrades were arrested here. One time, however, she evaded escape by hiding in a nearby stable. At 4 in the morning, Edgar Lansbury turned up with a wood cart, put Sylvia in a sack, hid her under the wood and smuggled her out of the East End.

Walk on a further few hundred yards till you reach the corner of Addington Street.

Stop 4
This is Bow Road Police Station in which Sylvia and her allies were often held before being carted off to prison. At the back there are still stables for police horses, the descendants of those who were used to break up suffragette demonstrations.

Continue to walk along Bow Road until you reach Alfred Street on your right.

Stop 5
On the building in front of you is the Minnie Lansbury Memorial Clock, the only monument to Minnie in the area. The plaques talk of her as an East End suffragette, champion of local people and a life devoted to the poor of the Borough.

Keep walking on and soon you reach Lansbury House.

Stop 6
This marks the site of George Lansbury's house where he lived until his death. Council flats now stand on the site as the house was bombed in the Blitz. That's entirely appropriate as George was a great defender of the need for councils to improve local housing.

Keep walking down Bow Road. Across the Bow Road you see a beautiful Italianate building. This used to be the City of London Union Workhouse and later became the St Clements Hospital which specialised in the treatment of mental health.

Turn right down Coborn Road and then turn left down Morgan Street. Soon you emerge into a square as beautiful as it is unexpected.

Stop 7
This is part of the Tredegar Estate named after the Morgan family who were the Barons of Tredegar; they had made their fortune from iron works in South Wales. They moved into property speculation and in the 1830's the family developed this estate in the hope that it would become the Belgravia of the East. It didn't. London was expanding rapidly and soon the square was surrounded by workers' housing and increasingly noxious industries. It was to take over 150 years for the area to regain its social cachet.

Go down Tredegar Terrace and then right down Lichfield Road to turn left down Coborn Street. Cross Antill Street and down Selwyn Road, almost opposite, and then into its continuation, Norman Grove.

Stop 8
At the end of Norman Grove at no. 45 there is a plaque announcing that this housed the East London Toy Factory with a babies nursery in the garden. It was surprisingly long-lived. Sylvia set this up in 1914 and it lasted for almost 30 years. The rationale at the beginning was clear: the outbreak of war meant many women had to get a job to make ends meet and feed themselves and their children. Sylvia stepped in where the state was tardy or non-existent. She employed the East End women to make sophisticated wooden

toys for West End stores. The wood, of course, came from Lansbury's timber yard. The women were paid a higher rate than in other local factories but their children still needed looking after while their mothers were at work. So Sylvia set up nurseries for them where the women could leave their children for a few pence and have them fed three meals a day. The plaque references Norah Smyth who financed many of Sylvia's activities. She spent all her wealth on the movement and by the end of her life was left destitute.

Carry on down Norman Grove and take a left onto Roman Road and then right. Stop at the traffic lights.

Stop 9

This is the heart of Bow and for a time it was the centre of Sylvia's activities. Much of it has been bombed or redeveloped and little survives from 100 years ago. In particular, Bow Baths has disappeared. It was able to hold up to 5,000 people and Sylvia used it to organise mass meetings of the suffragette movement. It was there she organised and launched the 'People's Army' in 1913 to protect demonstrations and meetings from the police. More peacefully, it was also where she organised a New Year's Party in 1916 for 900 local children.

Turn left down St. Stephen's Road and walk down towards Old Ford Road. On your left you'll be passing the site of George Lansbury's wood yard. When you get to the corner of Old Ford Road, move 10 yards to your right.

Stop 10

Opposite you will see a street named Gunmakers Lane and, where you're standing, was a pub called the Gunmakers' Arms. This was because there was a factory opposite which made guns and ammunition for the war effort. In 1915, Sylvia took over the pub, called it the Mothers' Arms, and turned it into a nursery, partly because the one at Norman Grove was full. It was run, for a time, by Minnie Lansbury.

Cross St. Stephen's Road and walk up Old Ford Road until you reach the Morpeth Arms.

11. The Women of Bow

Stop 11

On the far wall there is a tremendous mural featuring Sylvia Pankhurst and her work in the area. It's absolutely appropriate that it is here as the garden was where her headquarters were during the last part of the war. It housed a meeting hall, a nursery and a cost-price restaurant which served hundreds of poor East Londoners every day. It was also where she lived for many years until she moved out of the East End in 1924.

Carry on over the canal bridge and then into Victoria Park. Walk to your left till you get to Grove Road which intersects the park.

Stop 12

You're now at the entrance to the park which was where Sylvia's paper, the 'Women's Dreadnought' (later the Worker's Dreadnought') was regularly sold. It was also the end point for many of Sylvia's marches and where she used the open space for many of her mass meetings. These often ended in violence with the police employing tactics which would horrify us today. In May 1914, for instance, a demonstration of suffragettes ended here. 20 women had chained themselves to Sylvia to prevent her being arrested. The women were penned in by the police at the boating lake in front of you. Sylvia was arrested and the other women were then forced to run a gauntlet of baton-wielding police.

Across the little roundabout and to your left once stood the house where in May 1913 the East London Federation was formed.

But our walk is now over and it's time to leave this tiny area which was so important for the women's and Labour movement 100 years ago.

AND FINALLY

There is an excellent pub, the Crown, opposite our end point which overlooks the park.
  To get home, just walk down Grove Road to Mile End Station.

FURTHER EXCURSIONS

Recognition of these women is shamefully poor. An East End Women's Museum, based in Barking, was planned but currently seems stalled. A statue to Sylvia is due to be erected on Clerkenwell Green but that is dependent on planning permission. There is a committee aiming to celebrate the Match Girls with a statue but nothing is yet agreed. Eleanor is graced only with a plaque where she died and Minnie has only her clock. The work of the suffragettes, including Sylvia, features in the previous chapter. Eleanor is, of course, accorded a major role in the Marx walk in this volume, and her influence was strongly felt in the docks, so you could perhaps undertake one of the dock walks either in this volume or in my first guide.

12. THE SALTERS OF BERMONDSEY

On this walk, we trace the footsteps of a remarkable couple who lived in and helped transform Bermondsey in the first half of the 20th century. They were Ada and Alfred Salter who between them dominated the politics of the borough for 40 years.

Bermondsey, at the turn of the 20th century, was known as the kitchen of London. Every day, agricultural produce trundled up the Old Kent Road from the 'Garden of England' into London through Bermondsey. The area's docks imported foodstuffs from around the globe. This was then processed in the area to feed the ever-expanding London market. The industry was massive: 40% of jam and biscuits eaten in the UK, for instance, were made in Bermondsey. Some of the factories were enormous: Peek Frean, for instance, employed over 2,400 people, mainly women, in its Bermondsey factory. Other well known firms such as Hartley's jams, Sarson's Vinegar, Spillers dog food, Jacob's biscuits, Pierce Duff's custard and Crosse and Blackwell pickles were all made in the area. Another major Bermondsey industry in the area was leather making. Something like 40% of all leather goods produced in the UK were made in an area less than a half square mile in the middle of Bermondsey. It contained Europe's largest hat factory as well as hundreds of tiny firms employing a few people each.

Conditions in these factories ranged widely. At Peek Frean, for instance, there was a bank, fire station and post office on site, clubs and societies were set up and workers had access to free medical services. On the other hand, the fur and leather industry used noxious chemicals in their manufacturing processes, leading to diseases of the nervous system and thus bequeathing us the phrase 'mad as a hatter'. Wages, especially for women, were very low. While men could earn perhaps 80p to £1 a week at the beginning of the 20th century, women had to be content with around 40p and young girls only 15p. As a result, Bermondsey was an extraordinarily poor area, characterised by high infant mortality, poor education, very poor housing and rudimentary medical services.

It was in this environment that Ada and Alfred Salter began to work in the late 1890s.

She was a young, idealistic middle class woman who, like others of her generation, rejected the life of domestic respectability mapped out for her by society. Instead, she moved from the Midlands to the slums of London to try and improve the living conditions of the poor and, especially, of the young girls working in the food factories. Alfred was a local boy from Greenwich who had studied medicine at Guy's Hospital. He was one of the most promising students of his generation, winning medals for his scholarship. A glittering medical career beckoned but instead he committed himself to serving his local community. He began to work providing medical services to one of the missions in Bermondsey. There he and Ada met.

She converted him to Quakerism and he converted her to socialism. Armed with their new beliefs, they married and two years later had a daughter, Joyce. But their family life was marked by tragedy. The Salters always lived amongst the people of Bermondsey rather than commute in from the healthier suburbs. When she was 8, Joyce contracted scarlet fever and died. She was their only child.

The couple continued their work in the missions of Bermondsey for the rest of their lives. Alfred set about transforming medical services in Bermondsey. He set up a surgery with other idealistic doctors, each were paid the same small wage. Between them they introduced a rudimentary scheme of health insurance with the very poorest paying nothing at all. He also introduced a range of truly innovative measures into his practice. He set up travelling film shows in 'cinemotors' around the slums showing inhabitants how to avoid some of the diseases ravaging the area. These were extraordinarily popular with hundreds viewing the impromptu showings. He also set up the first council-funded solarium to help treat TB and also set up a sanatorium in the countryside where patients could get away from the pollution of South London. His efforts were successful. Rates for TB, child mortality and other diseases declined rapidly.

Ada continued to work amongst the women and girls of Bermondsey, trying to improve conditions in the local factories. She was centrally involved in the 'Bermondsey Uprising' of August 1911 where thousands of women workers struck for better pay, shorter hours and the right to join a union. By the end of the month, strikes had taken place in 21 factories, and in 18 of them, the women had won significant concessions. 4,000 women joined a union. Ada was at the centre of this movement, helping set up food distribution points to support the strikers and their families. She was also active in the suffragist movement. She rejected the violent tactics of Emmeline Pankhurst's Women's Social and Political Union preferring the more class-based politics of the Women's Freedom League. (For more on this issue see the chapter on the suffragettes).

The Salters realised that more was needed and political change necessary. So they increasingly turned to politics, setting up a branch of the Independent Labour Party in the area. In 1910, Ada was elected as the first woman councillor in London and in 1922 she became London's first woman mayor. Alfred became MP for the area, a position that he was to hold until the end of his life. Their vision for the area was nothing short of its transformation. Alfred wrote that *'We'll pull down three quarters of Bermondsey and build a garden city in its place'* and in their manifesto they wanted *'to make Bermondsey a fit place to live in ... to promote health, to lower the death rate and to increase the well-being ... of the 120,000 people who live here. ... We will cleanse, repair, rebuild and beautify it, make it a city of which all citizens can be proud. Bermondsey is your home and our home.'*

The council created a Beautification Committee which employed some 36 people to transform the area. 9,000 trees were planted and green spaces filled with flowers were created across the borough. Model houses were built which emphasised the need for light, space and greenery. This was a new way of looking at and dealing with slum areas. It was no longer just about remedying the most obvious problems; it was about creating a vision to aspire to. The 'Bermondsey Revolution', as it was called, became famous, appearing in magazines and papers and attracting visitors from Europe and North America. Ada went on to be elected to the London County Council where she fought for, and eventually gained, recognition of the concept of the Green Belt around London. As Bermondsey's MP throughout the 30's Alfred played a key role in the development of Labour Party policies. He was a founding member of the Socialist Medical Association which worked for the establishment of a National Health Service.

Ada died in 1942. Alfred wrote a month later: *'The loneliness grows deeper and has not lessened in the slightest with the lapse of time. Sometimes it is almost unbearable, but I have to learn to bear it.'* Alfred resigned his seat just before the landslide 1945 election which led to the creation of the NHS. He died shortly afterwards.

The Salters are still remembered in Bermondsey. There is a Salter Street, an Alfred Salter Primary School, a Salter Medical Centre and Salter Park. There are plaques, information boards, a complex of statues in Southwark and an annual lecture in their memory. Fitting memorials to two great lives.

FURTHER READING

There are few books devoted exclusively to the Salters. There is a biography by Fenner Brockway entitled *The Bermondsey Story: The Life of Alfred Salter* but that was written over 70 years ago. More information can be found in chapters of more general books such as 'Rebel Footprints' by Dave Rosenberg.

THE ROUTE

We start at London Bridge Station. From London Bridge walk south down Borough High Street and then turn left down St Thomas Street, noting the plaque on your right to John Keats who studied at Guy's. On your left there is the Old Operating Theatre which gives an insight into our medical past and makes you so thankful for the invention of anaesthetics. Turn into the entrance of Guy's Hospital.

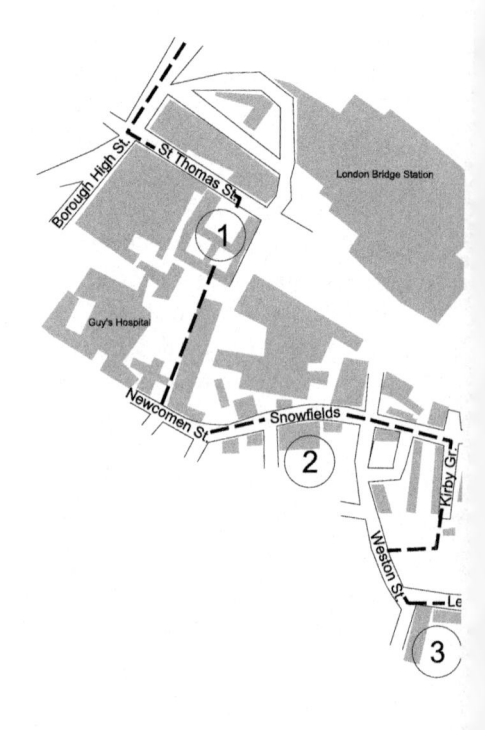

12. The Salters of Bermondsey 167

THE WALK

Our walk takes us from London Bridge through old Bermondsey and the places where the Salters worked, ending in the riverside village of Rotherhithe.

1. Guy's Hospital
2. Guinness Trust Buildings
3. Leather Exchange
4. Morocco Street
5. Bermondsey Street
6. Tanner Street Park
7. Time and Talents
8. St Mary Magdalen

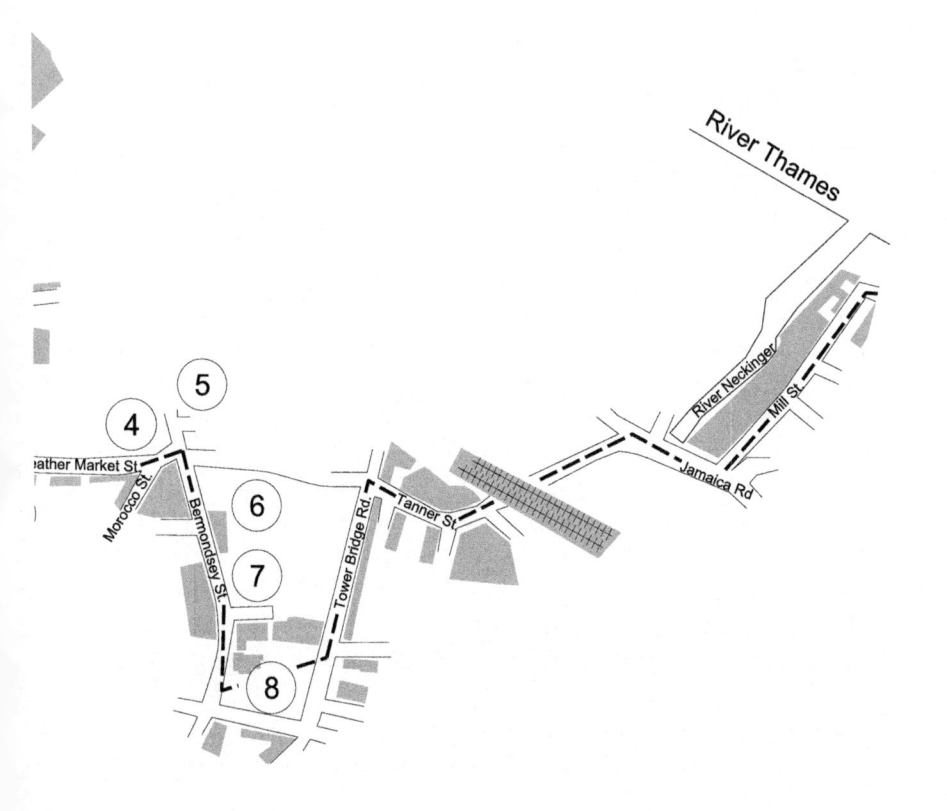

Stop 1

You are in the square of Guy's Hospital with a statue to Thomas Guy, the principal benefactor, in the centre. This is where Alfred Salter studied as a young medical student. He probably wouldn't have gone often to the beautiful chapel on the right side of the square as at this point in his life he had rejected religion. However, that's no excuse for you not to go and have a quick look. It has a memorial to Guy and some beautiful Arts and Crafts decorative panels.

Go through the colonnade at the end of the square. On your left there is a shelter which used to be part of Old London Bridge for travellers to take refuge from the wind and rain. Today it houses a statue of John Keats. Just beyond it is a plaque to one of Guy's most famous employees – Ludwig Wittgenstein. The great philosopher worked as a porter during the Second World War; he remained incognito as he was an Austrian national, so not a particularly popular nationality at the time.

Keep walking through the hospital and when you reach Newcomen Street, turn left and walk down Snowfields.

Stop 2

You come to two monuments to 19th century philanthropy. On your right is a fine example of the tenement blocks that were being built to house the poor. These are the 'industrial dwellings' or '4%ers', so called because the rents were supposed to return 4% on the capital cost. These started appearing in the East End during the 1880s and were often financed by wealthy benefactors such as Rothschild or Peabody. Here, it was the Guinness family that built the blocks in front of you. While these marked a revolution in the living conditions of the poor in that they provided heat, water and shelter at reasonable rents, Ada Salter recognised their limitations. They were necessarily cramped and light and air could be at a premium. Ada wanted to revolutionise the expectations of the community and to provide houses of which everyone could be proud.

On your left you will see our first example of a mission building. These were often Christian-inspired and undertook evangelical and social work in the slums of

London to help the poor. The building is marked with a plaque and commemorates the work of Arthur's Mission in 1865. It used to house a 'Ragged School' where the poor could access an education.

Take a right turn down Kirby Grove along the side of the Guinness housing and into the small park at the bottom. Bear right out of the park and turn left into Weston Street.

Stop 3
The grand building in the corner is the Leather Exchange, the centre for the leather trade in Bermondsey where leather in all its forms was bought and sold. Around the outside are some fine plaques which describe the leather making process from beginning to end. It's worth popping into the central square by going through an atmospheric entrance a few yards down Weston Street. With a vivid imagination, it's just about possible to recreate the bustle that once must have been here with the carts carrying skins in and leather out.

Go down Leathermarket Street along the front of the exchange and stop at the intersection with Morocco Street.

Stop 4
Morocco Street is named after a particular type of leather mainly used in book binding. You can see the ghostly reminders of the leather trade all around. Many of the buildings were warehouses holding stocks of leather. Opposite there's a strange little garage but look carefully and at the sides you will see two horses'

heads attesting to its previous use as stables and blacksmiths.

A few steps on and you reach Bermondsey Street.

Stop 5

Bermondsey Street was originally a Roman causeway leading through the marshes towards London Bridge. Recently it has seen an extraordinary revival, full of expensive delis, coffee shops and gourmet pubs. It is a place of enormous contrasts; a few hundred yards to your left there are some houses dating back to the 16th century. They stand almost opposite Zandra Rhodes' modernist Fashion and Textile Museum.

Turn right and just opposite you is Tanner Street Park.

Stop 6

This park was created by Ada Salter in the 1920's. It replaces the Bermondsey Workhouse, perhaps the most hated institution in Victorian society. The workhouse was where the old and poor were housed if they could not work. Conditions inside were supposed to be no better than those outside to dissuade the poor from being a burden on the ratepayers. Families were separated into men, women and children and set to work. The Bermondsey Workhouse survived for 150 years despite one report saying that the infirm wards were *'a fever nest'*, the sanitary arrangements being *'scandalously bad'*, the accommodation for tramps being *'not fit for a dog.'* The workhouse was a place of terror for the poor, somewhere to be avoided at almost any cost, and so it was a deeply symbolic act for Ada Salter to order it be demolished and a park to be constructed in its place.

Start walking up Bermondsey Street.

On your right you'll pass the White Cube Gallery, one of London's leading venues for contemporary art. Shortly after, on your left at no. 169, you'll see what was once the largest hat making company in the world. Christy & Co employed at its peak 500 workers in this plant.

Further up on your left a handsome building is labelled Time and Talents in fine Arts and Crafts lettering.

Stop 7

This was a mission founded by Anglican women who wanted to help young middle class girls do something useful with their often sheltered lives. They offered opportunities to volunteer to work with young factory women and offer their 'time' and 'talent.' The organisation did a great deal of good. It set up, for instance, a hostel for factory girls so they could move out of cramped and unsanitary rooms into a safe environment. It also ran social clubs offering singing, dancing and teaching the girls to read. It is still going strong today and we'll pass its current centre later on. Ada was involved in a similar mission in the slums near Bloomsbury before moving south of the river.

A few steps further on the left you come to the parish church of Bermondsey.

Stop 8

This is St Mary Magdalen. Originally it was built for the workers of Bermondsey Abbey founded in 1080, although the current building dates back to 1680.

Walk through the churchyard, noting the watch house at its entrance. This was to guard against the threat of grave robbers or 'Resurrection Men.' They would dig up freshly buried corpses to sell to the surgeons of the London hospitals who were teaching the new science of anatomy. One of the tombs the robbers didn't raid was the handsome memorial on your right where the Rolls family (of Rolls Royce fame) are buried. Walk through the churchyard and then turn left up Tower Bridge Road.

This was the scene of clashes in the 1911 Women's Strikes where Ada was so prominently involved. Turn right down Tanner Street. (The old Sarson Vinegar factory is on the opposite corner.)

You come out at Dock Head. Take a second to look over the brick wall in front of you for an unexpected view down the River Neckinger, one of the 'lost' rivers of London.

Turn right down Jamaica Road. A little further along this road was the site of Alfred's first surgery which revolutionised health care in Bermondsey. Take the first left down Mill Street and at the bottom turn right down Bermondsey Wall.

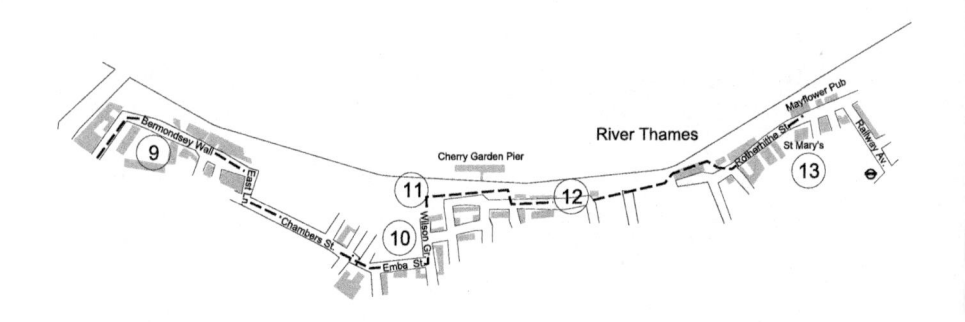

9. Jacob's Island

10. Wilson Grove

11. Cherry Garden Pier

12. Salter Statues

13. St Mary's Churchyard

Stop 9

You are now in what used to be Jacob's Island, one of the most notorious slums in London. It was an island, surrounded by water on three sides, and Dickens called it the 'Capital of Cholera' given the terrible hygiene. He set the climactic scene of Oliver Twist on the Island where Bill Sykes, after having killed Nancy, found himself surrounded by pursuers. He tried to swing himself to safety from the roof but was shot and only succeeded in hanging himself. Little remains from this time, although there is a nice water feature in the luxury flats you walk past to remind the inhabitants that they would have once lived on a cholera- and crime-ridden island.

Walk down Bermondsey Wall, turn right at East Lane, left down Chambers Street until you reach Riverside Primary School. At the far end of the school was the mission founded by John Scott Lidgett, a prominent Methodist theologian. This is where Ada and Alfred first met and worked together. The settlement offered a wide range of services including health, education and leisure activities. Ada was in charge of the girls' club which catered for young factory workers.

Walk down Emba Street in front of you and stop at the corner with Wilson Grove.

Stop 10

The houses you see around you are exemplars built by Ada Salter to demonstrate what she wanted for the people of Bermondsey. They are airy, light and surrounded by greenery. They sum up her philosophy of what housing should be like; not just about slum clearance but about creating an environment where families could flourish. Visitors often comment that the houses remind them of the model new towns around London rather than what they would expect in the inner-city. It's a very apt comment as Ada went on to become a member of the London County Council and was one of the leaders of the movement for the creation of new towns and the Green Belt.

Turn left down Wilson Grove until you reach the river at Cherry Garden Pier. There is a wonderful view of London in front of you; stretching from the skyscrapers of Canary Wharf in the east to Tower Bridge and the City in the west.

Stop 11

Cherry Garden Pier is named after the cherry trees that the monks of Bermondsey Abbey planted here. They were visited by Pepys who patronised the inn on Jamaica Road and strolled in the orchards and watched his maids play.

It's also where J M W Turner painted his most famous picture, The Fighting Temeraire. This was voted the nation's favourite painting and currently adorns our £20 note. The picture shows the great ship, which had been one of the victors at the battle of Trafalgar, being towed by a tiny steam tug to Rotherhithe at sunset. There the ship would be broken up and so the painting symbolises the end of the old and glorious British Navy and the inexorable rise of steam power. At the time, Turner was living incognito with one of his mistresses in a pub just across the river in Wapping.

Turner took a great deal of artistic licence in the painting. There were three in particular: the ship was known by its crew as 'The Saucy Temeraire', (not a particularly heroic title for the great painting, so Turner changed the name). The ship had also been used as a prison hulk for the previous 20 years and no longer possessed its guns or masts, in fact it was just that – a hulk – but Turner took it back to its former glory. Finally, Turner had the temerity of having the sun set behind the ship: the problem is that it's coming upstream so the sun is setting in the east! Apart from that, it was a pretty accurate representation of the scene. If you look carefully at the background of the painting, you can just about make out the riverside view in front of you of the warehouses of Rotherhithe.

Walk to your right along the river bank, passing a fine victorian wharf, and a warehouse with the date 1934 on it reminding us that the area was heavily dependent on dock work up to the Second World War and beyond.

On your right, you pass some social housing dating from the early 20th century, another example of the 'Industrial Dwellings' movement.

The street opens up in front of you to another wonderful vista of the river. Before you walk over to admire the view, look to your right to see the remains of an archaeological site: a manor house belonging to Edward III dating back to the mid-14th century. It was here that Wat Tyler and Jack Straw came to negotiate with Richard II during the Peasants' Revolt of 1384. It wasn't successful; the king took one look at his revolting subjects and fled back to the safety of the tower.

Stop 12

Overlooking the river is an ensemble of four statues. It's entitled 'Dr Salter's Daydream' and shows an elderly Alfred sitting on a bench thinking back over his life. To his left stands Ada in her fine Edwardian dress but holding a spade symbolising her efforts at transforming Bermondsey. By the wall is Joyce, accompanied by her cat.

An original statue of Alfred was erected in 1991 but stolen, presumably for its bronze content. A public subscription backed by the council rapidly raised the funds to reinstate it and this time it gave rightful recognition to Ada.

Continue walking along the riverbank for a further few hundred yards until you reach the boundary between Rotherhithe and Bermondsey. In a garden on your left a statue of a small Indian elephant looks down on you. This is highly symbolic as Rotherhithe was once a base for the ships of the East India Company. As you walk down Rotherhithe Street, on your left you'll need a bit of imagination, but you can almost think yourself back to the heyday of the town in the 18th and 19th centuries. Much of the architecture is original, although the warehouses are now converted into flats. But the features of a dockland community still remain; the cranes, gangways, the yards where carts were laden with produce to be taken into central London. Some of the names too remain: you'll find Bombay Wharf and East India Court.

Rotherhithe Street opens up into St Mary's Churchyard.

Stop 13

This is one of the most historic places in South East London and there is so much to see. There has been a church on the site since at least the 13th century, but Roman remains have been found, so the settlement may be much older. St Mary's itself was rebuilt in 1715 after the original church was damaged by flooding. If it's open it's well worth looking inside; some of the timbers from the Temeraire were made into a bishop's chair and table and Captain Christopher Jones, the captain of the Mayflower, is buried by the altar.

Across from the church is a fine old charity school dating from the early 18th century where the children of the sailors who set forth from Rotherhithe were guaranteed a basic education. Note the two statues of children in blue coats. At the time blue was a cheap dye and so it was normally adopted for the uniforms of charity schools. Hence the preponderance of bluecoat schools.

Next to the school is a small building, now a café, with a plaque dating it to 1821. This is another of the original watchhouses in London. This is slightly different from the one we saw earlier in our walk. It has windows both at the front and the back as it was built to protect not one, but two, graveyards. At the back is a low building which used to be a mortuary, one of the largest in London, which dealt with the unfortunates who ended up in the river. Today it is the base for the 'Time and Talents' organisation whose original building we saw earlier on.

There are two memorials in the main churchyard which are well worth seeking out. The first is a statue of Christopher Jones, the captain of the Mayflower. He set sail from Rotherhithe in 1620 to pick up the 'Pilgrim Fathers' and take them off to Massachusetts. He's looking somewhat wistfully back to the Old World while holding the new in his brawny arms.

Close by there is a tomb with an iron fence around it. This holds the body of Captain Henry Wilson who gave his name to the street where we saw Ada's houses. But it also contains a very poignant story. The inscriptions tell us how Wilson was shipwrecked in Palau in the South Seas while exploring on behalf of the East India Company. He was rescued by a local ruler whose son, Lee Boo, Wilson brought back to London. The idea was that Lee Boo could take western technology back to his island home. Lee Boo was a sensation when he arrived in London; he was called 'the Black Prince' by London society who flocked to meet him. But, of course, it ended in tragedy. Lee Boo caught small pox and died within three months. He was only 20. However, no-one told the inhabitants of Palau that their future ruler was dead. For years there was a supposed king over the water who, one day, would return to lead the island into the modern world. There is one last twist to this sad tale. Over 200 years later, just across the Thames in Stratford, Palau sent their first delegation to the Olympic Games in 2012. Their flag-bearer was a man dressed in late 18th century fashion. Lee Boo had finally returned to lead his people into the modern world.

And with that our story, and our book, comes to an end.

AND FINALLY

There is only one place to go and that is the Mayflower pub, just by the church. It's one of the great London pubs with fantastic views. It has got a brilliant deck over the river, although at high tide you run the risk of wet feet. Just a fabulous place. The only problem is that the ghosts of the teetotal Salters probably won't join you.

Once you've finished, Rotherhithe Station is a few hundred yards away behind the museum.

FURTHER EXCURSIONS

You can easily spend the afternoon at Rotherhithe. Just round the corner is the Brunel Museum (which I covered in a previous chapter) and there's also the Sands Film Studio which has a Research Library with lots of rare photos relating to Rotherhithe and the docks. There are some fine cafés and lovely river walks.

ABOUT THE AUTHOR

Tim is a proud Londoner. After studying politics and history at the London School of Economics, he spent his working life in education. Since retiring, he has lectured on London's history to many different groups and regularly leads walks across the capital for Londoners and visitors alike. He can be contacted at **timpotter53@gmail.com**

His first book *Walking London's History* was published in 2020 and is available through **Amazon**.

Printed in Great Britain
by Amazon